REFLECTIONS

OF *God's*

Holy Land

Previously Published Titles

Miriam Feinberg Vamosh

Women at the Time of the Bible
Food at the Time of the Bible: From Adam's Apple to the Last Supper
Daily Life at the Time of Jesus
Israel, Land of the Bible
Pathways through the Land of the Hart

Eva Marie Everson

True Love
One True Vow
Shadow of Dreams
Summon the Shadows
Shadows of Light
Intimate Moments with God
Intimate Encounter with God
Silver & Gold
Sex, Lies, and the Media
Sex, Lies, and High School
The Potluck Club
The Potluck Club; Trouble's Brewing
The Potluck Club Takes the Cake

Forthcoming

The Potluck Catering Club (Book 1)
   August 2008
The Potluck Catering Club (Book 2)
   August 2009
The Potluck Catering Club (Book 3)
   August 2010

The Potluck Club Cookbook
Heels on Wood, Soles on Carpet
This Fine Life

REFLECTIONS
OF *God's* *Holy Land*

A PERSONAL JOURNEY THROUGH ISRAEL

Eva Marie Everson
&
Miriam Feinberg Vamosh

Published by
Thomas Nelson™
Since 1798

www.thomasnelson.com

Published in Nashville, Tennessee. Thomas Nelson is a trademark of Thomas Nelson, Inc.

Thomas Nelson, Inc. titles may be purchased in bulk for educational, business, fund-raising, or sales promotional use. For information, please e-mail SpecialMarkets@ThomasNelson.com.

Unless noted otherwise, all Scripture references are from The Holy Bible, New Century Version, © 1987, 1988, 1991 by Thomas Nelson, Inc. Other Scripture references are taken from the following sources: The Holy Bible, New International Version (NIV). Copyright ©1973, 1978, 1984, International Bible Society. Used by permission of Zondervan Bible Publishers. The King James Version of the Bible (KJV). Scripture quotations are taken from The New King James Version® (NKJV), copyright 1979, 1980, 1982, 1992 Thomas Nelson, Inc., Publishers.

Rabbinic quotations are taken from:
The Babylonian Talmud. London: Soncino Press 1935–1952. 34 vols.
Midrash Rabbah: Soncino Midrash Rabbah. Transl. and eds. H. Freedman and M. Simon. London: Soncino Press, 1951. 10 vols.
Quotes from the works of Josephus Flavius are taken from *The Works of Josephus*. Transl. William Whiston (Peabody, MA. Hendrickson, 1987).

Unless noted, photographs © and provided by Eva Marie Everson and Miriam Feinberg Vamosh. Additional photographs provided by Doron Nissim. More information on Mr. Nissim's work can be obtained at http://www.pbase.com/doronnissim/profile.

REFLECTIONS OF GOD'S HOLY LAND

ISBN 10: 0-8499-1956-8
ISBN 13: 978-0-8499-1956-5

Printed in the China
08 09 10 11 MT 9 8 7 6 5 4 3 2 1

Dedication

Eva Marie and Miriam dedicate this book in loving memory of
Dana Kempler
—1957–2007—
who brought us together in the Land of the Bible.
We love and miss you.
So very much.

. . . and to the late Danessa Feinberg,
who lived a life believing a work such as this could happen.

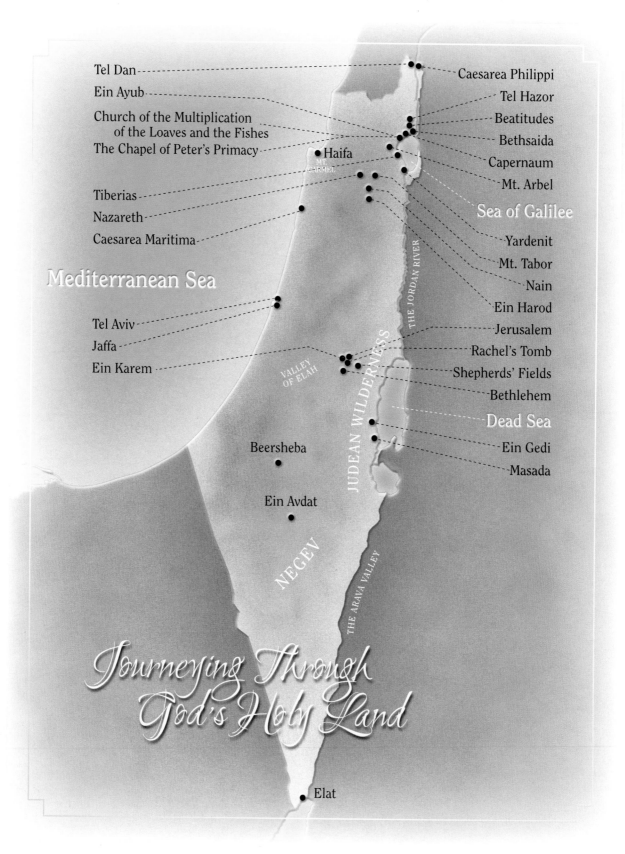

Tel Dan
Ein Ayub
Church of the Multiplication
of the Loaves and the Fishes
The Chapel of Peter's Primacy

Haifa
MT. CARMEL

Tiberias
Nazareth
Caesarea Maritima

Mediterranean Sea

Caesarea Philippi
Tel Hazor
Beatitudes
Bethsaida
Capernaum
Mt. Arbel

Sea of Galilee

Yardenit
Mt. Tabor
Nain
Ein Harod
Jerusalem
Rachel's Tomb
Shepherds' Fields
Bethlehem

Dead Sea

Ein Gedi
Masada

THE JORDAN RIVER

JUDEAN WILDERNESS

VALLEY
OF ELAH

Tel Aviv
Jaffa
Ein Karem

Beersheba

Ein Avdat

NEGEV

THE ARAVA VALLEY

Elat

*Journeying Through
God's Holy Land*

We write you now about what has always
existed, which we have heard, we have seen
with our own eyes, we have looked at, and
we have touched with our hands.
1 John 1:1

We write this to you so you can be full of joy with us.

Praise for Reflections of God's Holy Land

You've always wanted to go to the Holy Land, and this book will only deepen that longing. If for any reason you can't go, *Reflections of God's Holy Land* is the next best thing. You'll feel as if you've been there. Don't miss this.

> Jerry B. Jenkins
> Author, *Riven*
> The *Left Behind* Series

My journey through the Holy Land is etched in my memories. I had not expected to be so deeply moved by the experience. When I picked up *Reflections of God's Holy Land,* I was once again flooded with my "ancient" journey. If you've been to Israel don't miss this devotional experience, and if you've never been allow the authors to open for you a window of blessing. Capture for yourself *Reflections of God's Holy Land.* The view is spectacular! An ancient fireworks of beauty and truth. The research and photography alone are worth the price of this book."

> Patsy Clairmont
> Women of Faith® Speaker
> Author; *I Second That Emotion*

Having personally visited the land of the Bible over 100 times, I found *Reflections of God's Holy Land: A Personal Journey Through Israel* insightful and enlightening to read. Spectacular photos and wonderful words of meditation and reflections. If you have never seen the Holy Land in person or you have been there many times, you will find that this book will ignite your imagination of the origins of the Bible. A must for every living room and great for the whole family!

> Peter Sumrall
> President
> LeSEA Broadcasting

Reading *Reflections of God's Holy Land* reminds me of the privilege I had during my years in the United States of encouraging Christians to visit Israel. These beautiful pictures and moving words brought home to me once again that the relationship between our faiths is our common passion for the Bible and bond with the Land of the Bible. Our beloved friend Dana, to whom this book is dedicated, worked devotedly to show Israel's vital spiritual essence, and continues to live within the pages of this book. I know that *Reflections of God's Holy Land* will bless many with the knowledge of Israel, and I invite people to visit and see how easy it is to fall in love with the country.

> Mina Ganem
> Former Director
> Israel Government Tourist Office
> Los Angeles

The exquisite colors, perfect framing, and intelligent venues contained in the photos make it a "must-have" for anyone interested in Israel. And, if you weren't interested in the Holy Land before opening its cover, you certainly will be ready to hop on the next flight to Tel-Aviv before closing the final page of *Reflections of God's Holy Land.*

Miriam Feinberg Vamosh lends credibility and accuracy to the history and place descriptions contained on each page. Plus Eva Marie Everson's unique blend of journalist, Bible teacher, and excited tourist give her personal accounts an inimitable character I have not encountered in any book during my 30 plus years in Israel.

> Yuval Shomron
> Jerusalem Bureau Chief
> The High Adventure Global
> Broadcasting Network

In the Holy Land, the pages of Scripture come to life in an amazing way. *Reflections of God's Holy Land* is the next best thing to being in Israel itself! Beautiful photos and meaningful reflections will touch your heart and make the Bible much more real and close for you. This inspirational volume will be a treasure for you and your family for years to come.

Robert Stearns
Founder and Executive Director
Eagles' Wings (New York)

If you've been to Israel, this book will feel like a return trip. I highly recommend you settle in with a cup of something and experience the beauty and inspiration of these pages! I love it!!

Marilyn Meberg
Women of Faith® Speaker
and Author
Author, *Love Me Never Leave Me*

Reflections of God's Holy Land is a beautiful page-turning tour of the Holy Land. A great book for those who have wanted to experience Israel but have not traveled there. This book not only features the beauty of the country, but the emotion of the stories behind the historical scenery. More than a book—*Reflections of God's Holy Land* is an experience!

Debbie Alsdorf
Design4Living Ministries
Author, *Deeper: Living in the
    Reality of God's Love*
*Design4Living Bible Studies for
    Women*

If you've never been to Israel in person you can virtually go in the pages of this book. If you have gone before, the awakening to go again and again will tantalize your mind and stir your memory as you revisit the places and events that will last in your mind's eye forever. The written facts and nostalgia for the scenery will propel your longing for the peace of Home. I've walked the streets of the Holy Land, cried at the spirit of the sites, and suffered and rejoiced at some of the experiences in this great book. You can, too. Join with the authors on their journey, and you'll feel inspired, encouraged, and downright delighted to understand more about the homeland of the Master.

Dr. Thelma Wells, D.D.,
President, A Woman of God
    Ministries
Speaker, Extraordinary
    Conferences,
    formerly with Women of Faith®
Author and Mentor

I want to commend Eva Marie Everson, Miriam Feinberg Vamosh, and Thomas Nelson, Inc., for the beautifully published, *Reflections of God's Holy Land: A Personal Journey Through Israel*. Because the nation of Israel is constantly mischaracterized in the media, it is wonderful to see this beautifully illustrated book, combined with history and poetry, to capture the true essence of this anointed land. We are also living at a time when God is uniting Christians and Jews in an unprecedented way; how significant that you would unite two women, a Christian and a Jew, to capture fully the beauty of this land from each unique perspective. This book is a must for those who have traveled to the Land many times, or for those who dream about the day to come.

Laurie Cardoza-Moore
President
Proclaiming Justice to
    The Nations, Inc.

 was ironing my husband's shirt that beautiful September morning. He was in the shower and, in front of me, was the hotel room's television. It was kind of cool, I thought, watching *Good Morning, America*, knowing the ABC studio was just a few blocks away.

Then all hell broke loose.

Months later I received a phone call from a woman named Dana Kempler from IMOT (Israel Ministry of Tourism). She informed me I'd been chosen as a Christian journalist to go to Israel at IMOT's expense. Having heard in the news that there was some unrest there and having lived through the nightmare of New York City on 9/11, I declined the offer.

When my husband came home, I told him about the call. "What?" he asked. "You've wanted your whole life to go to Israel! You should go!"

He was right about that. As a Bible scholar and teacher, I'd more than "wanted" to go. I'd *yearned* to go. So, several weeks later, I packed my bags and—along with Dana and five other female Christian journalists—boarded an airplane heading for Tel Aviv. Upon our arrival we were met by a Jewish woman named Miriam

Feinberg Vamosh, then our guide and interpreter, now my dear friend.

Israel was nothing like the news channels reported it to be. With the negative press, Israel's tourism industry—which they depend on—was hurting. Expecting the truth from the media, I anticipated a bomb going off on every corner. Instead I was greeted with open arms by Jews, Christians, and Muslims alike.

Like most tours, ours went to biblical sites or the remnants thereof. A few days into the tour, we were taken to the ruins of Hazor (Tel Hazor), the only northern city burned to the ground by Joshua during the conquest of the Promised Land (Joshua 11:11). The morning was bright and sunny. We stood in an open field with the park's director, Mr. Hsein el Heib, who spoke in broken English and mostly Hebrew as Miriam interpreted for him. His love for Israel and especially for Tel Hazor was evident in the way he spoke about her and it, the way he looked over the land, the way he moved his hands—like the conductor of a fine orchestra.

Then he asked the question that would change my life. "We have found something interesting," he (according to Miriam) said, "We don't allow everyone to see it, but I would like for you to see it. Would you like to go and see?" There would be some difficult climbing down and up again, however. Three of us—along with Dana and Miriam—volunteered to go. After descending several centuries to the bottom level of the mound, we approached a wall covered by a blue tarp. Mr. el Heib's excitement increased as he neared it.

Mr. el Heib pulled back the tarp with his tanned hands. "This could be the soot from Joshua's fire," he proclaimed, pointing to darkened areas on the stone wall. We could, he said, touch it. The two other journalists went first. Then it was my turn. I felt a bit lightheaded, I admit. After all, as an Old Testament theology teacher, I taught about Joshua's bravery and the destruction of Hazor. But, this was not mere *words* about a fire. This could be the *evidence* of it.

I placed my hand on a low boulder to secure myself, then I reached my hand toward the wall. Dana aimed her camera as Mr. el Heib leaned toward me. "You are touching the Bible," he whispered in my ear, in as clear English as I've ever heard.

At that moment, I fell.

I don't know why. I just fell.

"Eva *falls* into the Bible," Dana quipped.

Mr. el Heib helped me up, and I dusted myself off. Moments later, I touched the Bible, truly *touched* the Bible, for the first time in my life.

Sure, I'd touched other things at other sites. But this was understanding *and* touching all at once. This was *me* "getting it."

That night I wrote in my journal: *Today I fell into the Bible. Literally. And in love with God all over again.*

You see, I discovered in that moment of falling that if Joshua's fire was such that some say it left these sooty remains after all these thousands of years, I wanted to know—to truly know—that the Holy Spirit's fire was so strong within me, that were my bones to be discovered thousands of years from now, the evidence of his dwelling within me would remain.

From that moment on, nothing in Israel looked the same. Every site, every stone, every trickle of water and city skyline had a spiritual message just for me. I journaled myself silly. At one point, as we walked along the Old City wall of Jerusalem, I said to Miriam (a human fount of knowledge), "Miriam, we should write a book together! You can give the facts, and I'll talk about what happens to people in the deepest part of their spirits when they come here."

Four and a half years later, I returned to the land of the Bible for the research Miriam and I would need to write this book. What began as a slip of my foot, a casual comment, and then a dream nearly lost, became a reality. As the plane pointed eastward, making its way toward the Ben Gurion Airport in Tel Aviv, my heart pounded. I was going *home;* for as anyone who has ever visited Israel will tell you, once you've gone, you will know where home truly is.

And one visit will never be enough.

That said, I know that—for a vast number of reasons—many who desire to go to Israel will not be able to make it. This book is for you. It is designed to allow you to see the sites through the Scriptures and photographs, hear the words of a gifted tour guide, and then—along with me—experience the spiritual revelations unique to Israel's sacred destinations.

It is also for those who have been to Israel or who are going to Israel, either for the first time or again. Together, we—you, Miriam, and I—will see and touch the Bible.

And none of us will ever be the same again.

Contents

From the Beginning to the End: Jerusalem!

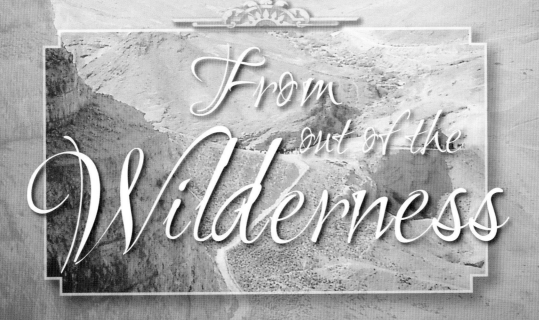

From out of the Wilderness

In the first month all the people of Israel arrived at the Desert of Zin, and they stayed at Kadesh. There Miriam died and was buried. There was no water for the people, so they came together against Moses and Aaron. They argued with Moses and said, "We should have died in front of the LORD as our brothers did. Why did you bring the LORD's people into this desert? Are we and our animals to die here? Why did you bring us from Egypt to this terrible place? It has no grain, figs, grapevines, or pomegranates, and there's no water to drink!" So Moses and Aaron left the people and went to the entrance of the Meeting Tent. There they bowed facedown, and the glory of the LORD appeared to them. The LORD said to Moses, "Take your walking stick, and you and your brother Aaron should gather the people. Speak to that rock in front of them so that its water will flow from it."

Numbers 20:1–8a

The desert and dry land will become happy; the desert will be glad and will produce flowers. Like a flower, it will have many blooms. It will show its happiness, as if it were shouting with joy. It will be beautiful like the forest of Lebanon, as beautiful as the hill of Carmel and the Plain of Sharon. Everyone will see the glory of the LORD and the splendor of our God.

Isaiah 35:1–2

Jesus said, "If you only knew the free gift of God and who it is that is asking you for water, you would have asked him, and he would have given you living water . . . Everyone who drinks this water will be thirsty again, but whoever drinks the water I give will never be thirsty. The water I give will become a spring of water gushing up inside that person, giving eternal life." The woman said to him, "Sir, give me this water so I will never be thirsty again and will not have to come back here to get more water."

John 4:10, 13–15

Ein Avdat/Nahal Zin

Israeli students carefully make their way along a rocky path between canyon walls to the place where water flows from the rock.

ike the children of Israel, our journey toward the promise begins in the wilderness. There are powerful memories in the Wilderness of Zin—of Moses leading a tired people ever closer to their goal, striking a rock to slake their thirst; of the deaths of his elder sister and his brother. As we scan the tree-less slopes, sun-baked and unrelenting, we—like the Israelites—might think of nothing better to call this place than "terrible" (Numbers 20:5).

From the top of this plateau in the Negev, you seek unlikely but welcome shade beneath the thorny branches of an acacia tree. Your eyes sweep the dry riverbed of Nahal Zin which rises up out of the Wilderness of Zin from the Sinai beyond. Look east, to where winter's rushing waters still cut a swath all the way to "the border of Edom" and the traditional tomb of Aaron at Mount Hor. Look west, toward Kadesh, where Miriam died and was buried.

But it is not for the sake of memory that we begin in the wilderness. It is because in a world where every waking minute something is grabbing for our attention, for once we are captivated by something that we have to seek out. A place that does not reveal its true face unless you are willing to find your way beyond the boundary of the desolation, and beyond your own limitations.

In the Wilderness of Zin, "there was no water for the community . . ." (Numbers 20:2 NIV). You have come here to go back to basics—to return to a place where that which flows effortlessly out of your tap is no less than a miracle. The ancient Jewish sages saw a powerful connection between Miriam's death and the Israelites' cries for water that went beyond their actual location. They imagined that Miriam continued to watch over them as she had watched over Moses in the bulrushes, providing them with water in time of need. Her connection with water is so close, that to this day legend associates a mysterious spring that bubbles up in the Sea of Galilee with Moses' elder sister.

You have to walk a rocky path to Ein Avdat, the spring that flows deep among the crags on the southwestern reaches of Nahal Zin where rainfall seeping and trickling through the rocks has found a weak place to burst forth. It is named after a city in the Negev where two thousand years ago the Nabateans learned to

---

The tomb of "Israel's George Washington," David Ben-Gurion (1886-1973) overlooks the Zin Wilderness. As Israel's first prime minister, he could have chosen to be interred on Mount Herzl in Jerusalem, alongside many of the country's leaders. Instead, he chose this magnificent Negev outlook because he wanted people to know in this special way how much he believed the desert would bloom, as the prophets had promised, and he saw in it the future of the Jewish people in their homeland. He was not a religious man in the ordinary sense, but he kept the words of the prophets on index cards under the glass on his desk. "In Israel, in order to be a realist," Ben-Gurion is quoted as saying, "you must believe in miracles."

Left: Ein Avdat's waterfall trickles from a mysterious source to a pool below.

Below: A guide checks on hikers who have braved the heights of Avdat.

conserve the tiny amounts of rainfall (fewer than ten inches in an average year) this region receives.

When you arrive at the spring, you read with new eyes: "Restore our fortunes, O Lord, like streams in the Negev." (Psalm 126:4 NIV). And you know that when the Hebrew prophets, John the Baptist, and Jesus turned to the wilderness for inspiration, they turned "living water" into a powerful and enduring symbol of salvation and joy.

Reflections

I am thirsty. The desert sun is blazing over my head, just atop the canyon walls. I stop along the rocky path long enough to look up, to gauge its position. How much longer, I wonder, before it dips behind the jagged cliff? How much longer before I reach the water that cascades from the rock?

The water-and time-altered canyon walls reflect majestically in a shimmering pool of water.

When I begin my trek again, it is only to look at the feet of the one walking ahead of me. The path he takes, I take. The rock he steps upon, I step upon.

A single thought comes to mind and—taking my eyes off the one before me—I turn to speak it to the one behind me. I slip; the earth's sand shifts under my feet, and I quickly turn forward again, vowing to keep silent until I find my way to the promised water.

Before long it comes. At first as trickling over stones, flat and almost level with the earth. Then as a rush, spilling to a pool below.

I step up, up, up until I come to the shade cast by walls of cool stone. I press my back against them and look up once more, to the place where the eagle stretches out his wings and soars in the sun's rays. I turn my head to the west and catch the rays as they dance across the rocks and up to where the water appears to begin. When I look away to where the pool ends and the stream begins, I see a reflection of the mountain, mighty and strong.

Mysteriously—though not a single drop of water has crossed my parched lips—I am no longer thirsty. "This is the way of it," the Lord whispers in the breeze. "This is the way of life. There are valleys so deep they have carved themselves far into the rock. You feel dry, nearly without

the strength to carry on. But you keep your eyes on the one who walks ahead of you, and the pathway becomes clearly marked. Easy to navigate. Take your eyes away—even for a moment—and you slip. You may even fall.

"But that's OK. You can always stand up—do you see my hand as it reaches for yours? Brush the dust away, and continue forward.

"Forward, to the rock that is higher than you. Higher, to the water that pours itself upon a dry and weary land. Up, to where the eagle soars and the sun dances, sending the mountain's reflection to where the water flows, and flows, and flows until it reaches the place where you began. The place where you will return again."

"Why did I have to come here?" I ask him.

"You came to see the Rock," he says. "To behold the source of the water. Understand this, and you need not be thirsty again."

Above: *The sun's rays dance across the rocks above a dark pool of water.*

As John's followers were leaving, Jesus began talking to the people about John. Jesus said, "What did you go out into the desert to see? A reed blown by the wind? What did you go out to see? A man dressed in fine clothes? No, those who wear fine clothes live in kings' palaces. So why did you go out?"

Matthew 11:7–9a

Judean Wilderness

Millennia of floods have carved these gulches through the marl badlands along the Dead Sea coast.

he time of Jesus was a time of oppression and confusion that touched every aspect of the lives of the spiritually hungry people who heard his message. If you were a well-connected friend of the rulers, a "Herodian" (Matthew 22:16), you might feel relatively secure behind the high walls of your estate, unless you or your family were threatened by tax-weary tenants (Matthew 21:35). If you were a Sadducee, a priest, or a Levite, you could take refuge in social status and in carrying out the work of the Temple, although you, too, had a growing worry: the extremists among your own people, frustrated at your life of privilege. If you were a Pharisee, you strove to teach the people the Bible at eye-level, but you had rivals—like the Sadducees—eyeing you suspiciously lest you reveal new doctrine, such as the resurrection of the dead.

In such an atmosphere, charged with spiritual and earthly tensions, even some of your own might revile you. But whether you were priest or peasant, you could not help but sense the heavy boot of Rome poised above your neck, this master of the land, its people, and even its king.

In a time when many people spent their entire lives within walking distance of their front doors, where could you go to escape this chaos? There was such a place. The Hebrew prophets sought their inspiration there; John's followers went to him out where the wilderness meets the Jordan River; Jesus fasted there for forty days, surrounded by flat, chalky, pita-shaped rocks that the devil taunted him to turn into bread (Luke 4:2–3). The Essenes, another group of seekers in those days, had also found it.

It was a place where you could meet with like-minded people, study Scripture, hear the interpretations of a gifted teacher, and listen for the still, small voice that Elijah heard after the storm had passed, a voice too often drowned out in the raucousness of ancient Judean cities, especially Jerusalem. You may have first longed for it after you followed the priests there to witness a goat,

Left page: The slightest moisture drifting eastward beyond the rain-shadow in Jerusalem turns the Judean wilderness hillsides into a feast of green for sheep and goats.

Below: Paths like these on a Judean Desert hillside, carved by carefully treading goats and sheep circling down to the desert springs, are the image of Psalm 23's "paths of righteousness."

the scapegoat, sent off a rocky cliff, bearing the sins of the people (Leviticus 16:21).

The Hebrew language has many nuanced names for arid land because the language was born in such a place. Not all such regions are a "land where no one lives, [a] desert that has no one in it" (Job 38:26). There were deserts, as we might imagine them, but there were also "parched lands," and "wilderness" (Isaiah 35:1 NIV).

If you lived in Jerusalem, Bethel, Bethlehem, Hebron, or Beersheba, the wilderness was right at your back door. A day's walk eastward could get you there; you could "go out into the desert to see" (Matthew 11:7; Luke 7:24) for a week, a month, or a year, and return spiritually revitalized, share your vision with others, and seek to build a new and better world.

he Judean Wilderness comes unexpectedly; our car rounds a bend in the road, and there it is, looming in the distance. And it is nothing I ever expected it to be.

I am anticipating flatlands. In my mind's eye, this is the way I have pictured it a thousand times. Hazy, with an ocean of shifting sands swept up by the occasional yet brutal wind, curling them toward the sky. I have pictured John the Baptist—thick-bearded with unruly hair—clad as a prophet, coming out of it. He shouts like a madman as he calls for man's repentance and return to relationship with God. I have envisioned Jesus—dressed in simple linen loosely billowing from squared shoulders, his head held high as he enters the wilderness.

But this I did not expect. Endless immense waves of sand-colored mountains, rounded in some places and peaked in others. One after the other, they roll on as though connected by their bases.

"This is where you came?" I ask Jesus out loud, long before I realize I have spoken.

"What did you come to the desert to see?" he whispers back to my soul.

It is a question that demands a response, but I cannot answer. Not right away. I don't know what I have come to see. I thought perhaps I had ventured here to understand where he had come to spend time in preparation with his Father. Time to connect what was behind to what lay ahead. A place of quiet shadows and vivid light.

But not this.

This is harsh. Demanding. Requiring more than simple steps onto the desert floor. This requires commitment. Fortitude. A desire to meet God and meet *with* God that permeates both body and soul.

This is no place for sissies. A reed swaying in the wind would soon be a reed broken and lying like a mat on the arid ground.

And so I wait. I do not dare attempt to come closer to a single one of these mountains without first being drawn to them. Drawn to their creator.

Drawn to mine.

In the distance I hear a bleating. I look and see a shepherdess walking along, her livestock following behind her, their focus diverted by temptations of both God and man. A tuft of grass here. A piece of trash there.

The shepherdess pauses, waiting for them to focus and draw near. They are, I decide, a lot like me. I follow my Shepherd. I get distracted by the temptations of both God and man.

But he always stops and turns around.

He always waits.

And, once again, I follow.

And it came to pass at that time that Abimelech and Phichol, the commander of his army, spoke to Abraham, saying, "God is with you in all that you do. Now therefore, swear to me by God that you will not deal falsely with me, with my offspring, or with my posterity; but that according to the kindness that I have done to you, you will do to me and to the land in which you have dwelt." And Abraham said, "I will swear." Then Abraham rebuked Abimelech because of a well of water which Abimelech's servants had seized. And Abimelech said, "I do not know who has done this thing; you did not tell me, nor had I heard of it until today." So Abraham took sheep and oxen and gave them to Abimelech, and the two of them made a covenant. And Abraham set seven ewe lambs of the flock by themselves. Then Abimelech asked Abraham, "What is the meaning of these seven ewe lambs which you have set by themselves?" And he said, "You will take these seven ewe lambs from my hand, that they may be my witness that I have dug this well." Therefore he called that place Beersheba, because the two of them swore an oath there. Thus they made a covenant at Beersheba. So Abimelech rose with Phichol, the commander of his army, and they returned to the land of the Philistines. Then Abraham planted a tamarisk tree in Beersheba, and there called on the name of the LORD, the Everlasting God. And Abraham stayed in the land of the Philistines many days.

Genesis 21:22–34 NKJV

Beersheba

This row of pillars once supported the roofs of Beersheba's storerooms from the time of the Kingdom of Judah.

"So, how did you two meet?"

"At the checkout counter . . ."

"At a church social . . ."

"We took the same class at college . . ."

"We were fixed up, and I was riding along on my camel, and I was so shocked the first time I saw him that I . . ."

"I was bringing my sheep to the well, and there he was, showing off again . . ."

Those last two boy-meets-girl stories are not exactly common these days. But at the well in Beersheba, it is as if Rebekah and Isaac, Rachel and Jacob, are there to tell you the beginnings of their love stories.

Beersheba is located on the southern end of the Patriarch's Highway, later to be the southern extent of Solomon's kingdom (1 Kings 4:25). Over the generations, Abraham and his clan of nomads plied this north-south mountain road that connected the bustling cities of Shechem, Bethel, Jerusalem, Mamre, and Hebron.

It was probably from Beersheba that Abraham sent his servant on the long journey northward to Aram-Naharaim (Genesis 24:10) to seek a bride for his son Isaac from among his kinsmen, as any self-respecting clan leader would have done to protect, enlarge, and enrich his family.

The people of ancient Beersheba dug their well centuries after Abraham's time. But as we peer down 210 feet to the now-dry bottom of this well outside the gate, or go down into the city's underground reservoir that channeled water from the stream, we can understand the strength, agility, and perseverance women in Bible days called on, day in and day out, to perform this most essential household task—drawing water.

That's how Abraham's servant knew the best place to seek a bride for his master's son. Rebekah not only met but exceeded his expectations. She rushed to help him and called him "my lord," even though he was dusty and disheveled from the road and could hardly have looked the part. She parted with some of the precious drinking water she had just drawn with her own hands or coaxed her donkey to pull up. Then she watered his camels, backbreaking work that could have taken hours to complete.

At the end of her long, camelback trip down the Patriarch's Highway to the Negev, Isaac's encampment shimmered into view, and Rebekah saw her future husband for the first time. Genesis 24:64 reads: *Rebekah also looked and saw Isaac. Then she jumped down from the camel.* However the English translation doesn't do it justice; the original Hebrew says that when Rebekah saw Isaac, she *fell off* the camel!

At the well of Beersheba, we recall another patriarchal suitor, Rebekah and Isaac's son Jacob, and his kinswoman bride Rachel (Genesis 29:2–12). If we turn to Exodus, we can picture Moses meeting his future sisters-in-law (and perhaps also his wife Zipporah) at the well. And Hagar, as Sarah's bondswoman, who was later cast out to wander "in the desert of Beersheba" (Genesis 21:14), would have come daily to a well like this to draw water for her mistress's household.

Like these women, Rebekah in her later life harnessed all the strength and determination she had first shown by the well, in the service of her family and their future.

Above: The highrises of modern Beersheba peek over the millennia-old mudbrick walls.

Left: Visitors descend some 60 feet via the ancient stepped shaft to Beersheba's main water system, which looks much as it did when it was abandoned 2,000 years ago.

31

At ancient Beersheba, the earth's sand crunches beneath my sandals, and the air is completely still. I approach the ancient city gate and I pause, my thoughts taken captive by the well, the tamarisk tree directly beside it, and the wide and flat land in front of it, dusty and green at the same time.

In the shimmer of the day's heat, I see what appears to be a figure walking in the distance, but—staring—I see that it is not one person, but two. Could it be Abraham, I wonder, with his wife Sarah, searching still for the city of God? Or is it Isaac walking along with his bride, Rebekah? And if so, what might they be talking about today?

I turn away, and I step into the ruins of the city, once neatly laid out with row upon row of large rocks laid one atop the other until it formed a place where governors resided and families dwelled. There men worked, and women drew water from a well so deep that my breath catches in my chest as I look down into it.

Today I choose to do what women of yesterday were forced to do: I descend down the seemingly endless stairs to the place where—once upon a time—water came by

way of a stream. The large stone steps are rough-hewn and steep; they carry with them the echoes of a billion footsteps. Inside the doorway that leads away from the sunlight and into the darkness, I am met by a wave of damp and cool air and the remembrance of young girls and water pots. Within these walls, I can hear their giggles and sighs as they talk about the boy they hope to marry someday.

And love enough to draw water for him.

I come out through another way and dare to look where I earlier saw the figures. They are gone, and I stand alone in a shady place, few and precious as they may be. I close my eyes and think of Rebekah, imagining her atop her camel, her back arched and hips swaying with each step it takes, carrying her to her new home. Her new life. Her new love. The sun begins its drop to the straight line of the horizon and, turning her head toward the south, she sees the man who will be her husband walking toward her. His neck stretches to observe the camels coming toward him, and she sees his face for the very first time.

"Who is that man?" Her words whisper across a single breeze.

"He is my master . . ."

My heart flutters and my eyes fly open. I run to the top of the sloping hill once more in search of a bride falling from her camel.

And I think, "When was the last time *your* Heavenly Bridegroom knocked you off your camel?"

Then I'm left to wonder how deep I'm willing to go each day to find water from the stream.

Above: *A modern-day shepherdess patiently waits as her flock grazes on the road to Beersheba.*

Left page: *"Abraham's Well" and the tamarisk tree at the entry to Tel Beersheba.*

Saul stopped chasing David and went to challenge the Philistines. That is why people call this place Rock of Parting. David also left the Desert of Maon and stayed in the hideouts of En Gedi.

1 Samuel 23:28–29

The smell of my perfume spreads out to the king on his couch. My lover is like a bag of myrrh that lies all night between my breasts. My lover is like a bunch of flowers from the vineyards at En Gedi. My darling, you are beautiful! Oh, you are beautiful, and your eyes are like doves.

Song of Solomon 1:12–15

You are my hiding place. You protect me from my troubles and fill me with songs of salvation.

Psalm 32:7

This covering will protect the people from the heat of the sun and will provide a safe place to hide from the storm and rain.

Isaiah 4:6

Ein Gedi

Life cascades
from this Ein Gedi
waterfall, bearing
rainwater from the
Judean Mountains.

ong before humans first came to Ein Gedi's overflowing spring, bountiful greenery provided sustenance and respite from the burning sun to the caprines and coneys of Psalm 104. Ein Gedi, or as the Bible calls it, "the Rocks of the Wild Goats" (1 Samuel 24:2), was David's oasis hideout and a place where he and Saul enjoyed a moment of healing in their rocky relationship.

The inhabitants of Ein Gedi eventually discovered a powerful secret of natural healing and beauty in a plant whose exact identity is a mystery to modern botanists. The ancients called it balsam, and it would change the history of the entire region. According to legend, it was among the gifts to King Solomon that the queen of Sheba brought from her homeland. To this day, *Boswellia sacra*, which might be a relative of balsam and from which frankincense is made, still grows there.

Some three hundred years after David's time, during the reign of King Josiah, the village of Ein Gedi was founded. The dry climate and fertile oasis were a perfectly balanced home for the "beds of spice yielding perfume" (Song of Solomon 5:13 NIV). The production process of what soon became a precious and prestigious commodity was so secret that even descriptions of the plant vary—some say it was a twelve-foot-tall tree; others say it was a shrub. Its alluring fragrance would have permeated the oasis, overcoming even the sweet scent of acacia blossoms. We do know its sap was extracted using a special knife, not made of iron. The wood, leaves, bark, and seeds were boiled with olive oil to distill an aromatic salve which, while expensive, was not as pricey as the resin. A pound of pure balsam cost as much as 1,000 silver denarii, an amount which scholars say would have taken three years of work to afford.

Balsam and other fragrances were often stored in alabaster jars, which were not only beautiful, but insulated the precious contents. The finest glass bottles containing perfume were dove-shaped and about four inches high. They were sealed by melting the glass, so the tail of the dove had to be broken to open them.

King Herod owned the balsam trade, whose revenues enabled him to carry out his grandiose building plans, including the Temple in Jerusalem. The cultivation of balsam at Ein Gedi, Jericho, and Zoar (a region south of the Dead

Caves dotting the walls of Ein Gedi like these once hid a fleeing David from King Saul's wrath and vengeance.

Sea; Genesis 13:10) continued in the Late Roman and Byzantine periods. But eventually, it disappeared. The synagogue of Ein Gedi, a stone's throw from the oasis, contains an enigmatic inscription that mentions the "secret of the village." Could this be a reference to the closely guarded production process of the precious perfume and salve? Excavations show that the village of Ein Gedi was destroyed in a fierce fire in the late sixth century AD and was abandoned forever. The inhabitants of this desert garden apparently took their secret to the grave.

hen I see Ein Gedi, I am captivated by its beauty—lush greens in the midst of desert mountains—and stunned by its height. Bone-weary from the sun, my mind turns to respite and, closing my eyes, I sleep long enough to again feel energy. No wonder this was David's hiding place—a refuge from harm and an overflowing sanctuary of God's presence and relief.

As I begin my climb toward David's Fall, a song rustles through palm fronds, and a canopy of sweet-smelling acacias welcomes me. I climb rocky steps, pausing long enough to engage in conversation with a coney, though I keep my distance. He is the color of the boulder upon which he sits, as though he's been here enough days to become as one with his oasis home. I turn to move on, and I am awestruck by the caves cut into the mountain's walls. I wonder in which of these did David hide while his adversary, Saul, crouched only a few feet away. But David, driven by love, spared the king's life.

I am again distracted by the rushing water of the small waterfall of Lower Wadi David. No one is there, so I step off the beaten path, balancing myself on large rocks and slipping my sandaled feet into the stream before coming to a rough embankment where I sit and ponder the way the emerald water falls and why I am drawn to it. It is both powerful and peaceful.

Later I return to the path and feel the sun as it warms my now damp skin. I sing the familiar psalm, "As the deer thirsts for streams of water, so I thirst for you" (Psalm 42:1), as I continue my climb through an archway of reeds towering over my head. I am nearing Upper Wadi David, the place where the largest waterfall drops to a small pool below. It sounds like the march of a mighty army.

In this place, a silent crowd gathers and admires the display of God's talents. They are a sharp contrast to the young men and women splashing about in the pools below, just as David's four hundred men might have done thousands of years ago.

Right here, right now, I feel connected to the heart of the man who sought after the heart of God. Though for a time David lived as a fugitive, he dwelt in the secret place of the Most High; so much so that when his enemy was vulnerable, he chose the right way. God's way.

I drop my head in shame. This is God's way, but too often not my way. I am not always willing to push my spiritual body in order to reach the water in the highest places. I find it easier to seek my own vengeance than God's power and peace. I choose to be apart from God rather than to live with him in such a way that—as the coney—I become one with my oasis home.

I look up once more and feel the spray against my face. I close my eyes and, drenched in his love, finish my psalm, "Your waves are crashing all around me . . . at night I have a song" (Psalm 42:7–8).

A playful coney makes his way down a boulder along the way to Upper Wadi David.

Above: The date palms of the modern-day oasis of Ein Gedi skirt the stark wilderness cliffs.

Left: The nimble creatures that gave Ein Gedi its name head across the "rocks of the wild goats," after a drink at the Ein Gedi spring.

Part of the people of Gad joined David at his stronghold in the desert. They were brave warriors trained for war and skilled with shields and spears. They were as fierce as lions and as fast as gazelles over the hills.

1 Chronicles 12:8

Control yourselves and be careful! The devil, your enemy, goes around like a roaring lion looking for someone to eat. Refuse to give in to him, by standing strong in your faith. You know that your Christian family all over the world is having the same kinds of suffering. And after you suffer for a short time, God, who gives all grace, will make everything right. He will make you strong and support you and keep you from falling. He called you to share in his glory in Christ, a glory that will continue forever. All power is his forever and ever. Amen.

1 Peter 5: 8–11

Masada

The table-mountain fortress of Masada rises, seemingly impregnable, from the Dead Sea Valley floor.

erod the Great is best known to Christians as the murderer of the innocent children of Bethlehem after he was informed that a king of the Jews had been born there (Matthew 2:16). Herod was crowned by the Romans, but his own subjects, the Judeans, saw him as an interloper. The Judeans' hatred of him caused him to order this massacre and to make other preparations to ensure his position.

Masada was one of a chain of fortresses Herod made ready so he could escape to friendlier lands from those who sought his downfall. He was not the first to fortify this craggy plateau. According to Flavius Josephus, the first century AD historian, Masada had been "built by our ancient kings." It may have even been the "stronghold" where David sought refuge from King Saul (1 Samuel 22:4).

When Herod was done with it, everything about Masada belied its bleak location on the edge of the Judean wilderness overlooking the Dead Sea. This same builder of Jerusalem's Temple and the showcase port of Caesarea spared no expense in hewing out Masada's water system, suspending its three-tiered palace impossibly from its northern face, and stocking its storehouses and armory.

In the decades that followed Herod's death, the harder Rome oppressed the Jews, the more its rule unraveled. Eventually, rebellion broke out against the empire. But sadly, Jewish factions were divided over how to respond to the Roman threat.

One of these factions was the Sicarii, whose name derived from the *sica*, a dagger they hid under their cloaks and did not shrink from using even among their own people. The extremist views of this group were rejected by their brethren. They were chased out of Jerusalem at the beginning of the revolt, in AD 66, and took refuge at Masada.

In the spring of AD 73 or 74, Jerusalem lay defeated, the Temple was in ashes, and the Romans were beating down the walls of Masada, the last rebel stronghold. It was the end of months under siege, and the rebels might have thought they were the only Jews left on earth. It was then their leader proposed that to preserve their freedom, they take their own lives and the lives of their families. When the Romans gained control of Masada, their victory must have been marred when they found the bodies of 960 men, women, and children. Among the dead, two women and five children were found alive and hiding inside a cistern.

The sages of the Talmud—who discussed every aspect of Jewish life in the first centuries—don't mention the events of Masada. Some scholars believe their silence was thunderous—a way of showing their disapproval of the choice the rebels made. In fact, the story of Masada was told only by Josephus, whose writings were preserved by the church, but virtually unknown to Jews until modern times.

Masada came into the limelight only with the return of the Jewish people to their land after the Holocaust and the rebirth of Israel, when it came to symbolize that the ultimate freedom was to cheat the oppressor. Everything else was shunted aside. It has only been in recent decades, as Israel faced new challenges at home and abroad, that views about Masada seem to be changing as some see a new lesson emerging: to avoid fighting a last battle in a war already lost, the greatest calling is to preserve unity, and thus, to preserve life.

Right page: *Visitors (bottom right) begin their trudge up the ramp the Romans built to conquer Masada 2,000 years ago.*

feel a tremor of excitement. We have driven past the Judean Mountains early in the day; their colors are various hues of tan and green. This vista will be breathtakingly different when the sun dips westward, sending its light to the rich blue of the sea, which paints the mountains in shades of rose and peach.

Then, out of the range, comes the distinctive table where Herod feasted and where shortly thereafter nearly a thousand Jews perished rather than be taken into slavery. Long before either, here, it is believed, David took refuge.

I become anxious to reach its crest and to drink in the lay of the land below. To see the lazy stretch of the Dead Sea disappearing southward into the rising haze and the waves of mountains that surround it. Masada, so lofty and proud with its squared skyline—beckons by virtue of its opulence—evident even in the midst of ruins—its safekeeping, and its tragedy in losing both.

Atop Masada, the sun bakes my skin. I feel tiny beads of moisture along my arms and on my face. I smell both sand and sweat; they blend with the pure air, and I'm surprised by the pleasant combination. Somewhere near the western edge of Herod's great hideaway is a pyramid of enormous ball-shaped rocks—Rome's artillery. They serve as a reminder of the siege that cost the Sicarii their lives. Peering to the earth's floor below, I gaze in fascination at the ramp built by the Roman soldiers determined to reach their captives. Scattered around Masada's base are the reminders of the enemy encampments. The Sicarii were surrounded.

Staring out the jagged remains of an ancient palatial window to the grandeur of God's landscape, I pause to think about how I might feel if, day after day, my enemy worked in plain sight, tirelessly and contemptuously, in an effort to either kill me or make me a slave. How would I sleep knowing that, night after night, that same force was encamped around my safe haven?

I step away from the window and follow the pathway to a lavish bathhouse with frescoed walls. Here, in the cool luxury, I take in a sharp breath, knowing I am familiar with how it feels.

The devil, your enemy, goes around like a roaring lion looking for someone to eat. Refuse to give in to him, by standing strong in your faith (1 Peter 5:8b–9a).

Hundreds of years before Masada became David's stronghold, thousands before it became Herod's palace and the rebel Jews' deathbed, the prophetess Deborah sang in celebration of the battle she had led against Sisera, the commander of King Jabin, their Canaanite captor. She remembered how the Israelites yelled, "*Take captive your captives,*" to Barak, instigating the fight (Judges 5:12 NIV).

At Masada, the Holy Spirit now declares the same to me. *Put on the full armor of God, so that when . . . evil comes, you may be able to stand your ground, and after you have done everything . . . stand"* (Ephesians 6:13b NIV).

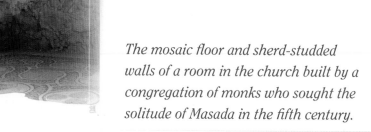

The mosaic floor and sherd-studded walls of a room in the church built by a congregation of monks who sought the solitude of Masada in the fifth century.

Above: *The square outlines of two Roman siege camps and part of the nine-foot-high wall they built to surround the Jewish rebels can still be seen from the top of Masada.*

Left: *Reconstructed double walls and floor of the "sauna" on Masada that King Herod may have used.*

45

Be merciful unto me, O God . . .
What time I am afraid, I will trust in
thee. In God I will praise his word, in
God I have put my trust . . . Thou tellest
my wanderings: put thou my tears into
thy bottle: are they not in thy book?
When I cry unto thee . . . this I know . . .
God is for me. In God will I praise his
word: in the Lord will I praise his word.
In God have I put my trust . . . Thy vows
are upon me, O God: I will render praises
unto thee. For thou hast delivered my
soul from death: wilt not thou deliver
my feet from falling, that I may walk
before God in the light of the living?

Excerpted from Psalm 56 KJV

The Dead Sea

Mount Sodom's wrinkled face looks itself in the mirror of the Dead Sea.

he Dead Sea slashes a dramatic path between the mountains of Judah to the west and Moab to the east. Most mornings, you can hardly see Moab, scene of the last leg of the Israelites' journey to the Promised Land and homeland of Ruth. But by afternoon, the clarity of the mountains' reflection on the sea's unruffled azure surface seems to plunge them right into the water and turn the world upside down. The opposing forces of nature are powerfully evident at every turn; there is no greater contrast than the Dead Sea against the backdrop of its cliffs and the green and welcoming splashes of the oases that surround its hot, dry shores.

The earth has never completely stopped moving and shaking in the Dead Sea Valley, which is part of the 3,700-mile long Syrian-African Rift. It has left us with the lowest place in the world and, with more than 30 percent salt and minerals, the most saline lake. It is the remnant of a gigantic lake that contracted, leaving scars in the soft, chalky rock, deep canyons in the harder limestone carved by winter floods, and Mount Sodom, made entirely of plaster-coated salt, the biblical backdrop of Lot's wife's last look at her homeland. Floods and springs from oases like Ein Gedi and the Jordan River continue to deposit fresh water into the Dead Sea. And with an evaporation rate of as much as 60 inches a year, the minerals and salt are left behind in dense concentrations.

Is the Dead Sea so salty nothing can live in it? That is what the Greek geographer, Pausanius, thought, and so he called it "the Dead Sea." But in the Bible, this lake is never called by that name. It's called the Salt Sea (Genesis 14:3 NIV) or the Eastern Sea (Ezekiel 47:18 NIV). And while Ezekiel's vision that the fish along its shores will be *as many as in the Great* [Mediterranean] *Sea* (Ezekiel 47:10 NIV) has not yet come true, about twenty-five years ago, Israeli scientists discovered the Dead Sea indeed has life. An algae—known as *donaliella*—thrives there and is a rich source of beta carotene now raised in pools of Red Sea water near Eilat, 100 miles to the south. The lake gives life in other ways: among its minerals is potash, a basic component of fertilizer. It also has bromide—a natural tranquilizer—and combinations of calcium, magnesium, and potassium that have made the Dead Sea the largest open-air spa in the world.

In antiquity the Dead Sea had several harbors. One, at Rujum el-Bahr in the north, may have even had a lighthouse standing on an artificial island. The harbors attest to the economic importance of the Dead Sea in antiquity: among other things, it was a source of salt, the most sought-after of condiments, and bitumen, used for caulking boats, medicines, and embalming in Egypt. Bitumen was still collected in modern times by the members of Kibbutz Ein Gedi in the 1960s.* The Dead Sea is still a source of riches—today it is mainly potash, used in fertilizers.

*Yizhar Hirschfeld, *Qumran in Context* (Peabody, MA: Hendrickson, 2004). 215.

In ancient times, kings and landed gentry sought the region's comfortable winter climate and built second homes there. Farmers working these estates at Ein Gedi and elsewhere produced priceless balsam, succulent dates, and other products. Salt, the most basic of seasonings, was in high demand, as was bitumen, which the Egyptians needed for embalming. Both minerals brought prosperity to the region and made the Dead Sea Valley a fascinating crossroads for people from all walks of life, as it is to this day.

Above: *The symbol of the Lord's promise turns the tide on a stormy Dead Sea day.*

Left: *A salty "stalagmite" stands sentinel on the Dead Sea's rocky shore.*

The sea is frighteningly beautiful, lying smooth as glass. It shimmers in the morning's blazing sun in an odd configuration of colors: psychedelic swirls of greens and blues with clusters of stark white at the shoreline. In the afternoon, the rugged mountains that rise on either side of the Dead Sea are mirrored in her calm water, so much so that I cannot tell where one begins and the other ends.

There is a gathering of bathers bobbing near the pebble-lined shore; the water is so dense that it keeps a human body afloat, no matter its size. Like the others who are drawn here for the healing balm of salt and black mud, I slip out of my sandals and step into the warmth of the water.

The water is clear and allows me to see my feet as though I'm looking through a window. Yet, with every little movement, I observe how rich in minerals this water truly is.

There are countless pebbles serving as a carpet for the Dead Sea. Like a child, I reach for one and, rubbing it between my fingers, am amazed at how creamy it feels. I let it slip from my fingers. It plops. I am both whimsical and foolish enough to then bring my fingertips to my lips. I shudder; no amount of warning could have prepared me for the level of salt now on my tongue.

These briny rocks on the Dead Sea shore look eerily like ice floes, until you see them shimmering in the 90-degree heat of a summer morning.

I look ahead, drinking in the sight of the noble hills of Moab, recording their beauty to memory. I turn to gaze over my shoulder and see the peaks of Ein Gedi and the Judean Mountains. Before me and behind me: mountains. I am so close to both, and yet I stand in the lowest place on earth.

I don't have to wonder or ponder what God is saying to me at the Dead Sea. I am all too aware of the mountaintop experiences in my life and the painful, tear-filled valleys in between. My tears have been caught and bottled. If this vista is any indication of God's craftsmanship, I can only imagine how intricate and fine my tear bottle, kept especially for me, must be.

Like the salty water in which I stand, the tears rising from my often-broken heart and pouring from my weeping eyes—even those accompanied by sobs as racking as the jagged cliffs around this sea—become the therapeutic balm my soul needs to carry on.

And so, like those who return to the healing sea, I will cry again before my Lord, knowing he will catch my tears and after a time of buoying in the palm of his hand, restore my wounded spirit.

Out of tiny Cave 4 in a marl spur near Qumran on the shores of the Dead Sea (bottom center) came thousands of fragments of the Dead Sea Scrolls.

From the House of Stone to the House of Bread

Jacob and his group left Bethel. Before they came to Ephrath, Rachel began giving birth to her baby, but she was having much trouble. When Rachel's nurse saw this, she said, "Don't be afraid, Rachel. You are giving birth to another son." Rachel gave birth to the son, but she herself died. As she lay dying, she named the boy Son of My Suffering, but Jacob called him Benjamin. Rachel was buried on the road to Ephrath, a district of Bethlehem, and Jacob set up a rock on her grave to honor her. That rock is still there.

Genesis 35:16–20

Rachel's Tomb

An Israeli soldier unlocks a gate leading to Rachel's Tomb, on the border between Israeli Jerusalem and Palestinian Bethlehem.

he irony is almost too painful to bear. Rachel, who pleaded "Give me children, or I will die," breathed her last by the side of the road between Bethel and Bethlehem after bringing Jacob's youngest, Benjamin, into the world. The last of the great trials of Rachel's tumultuous life left its mark on the generations that followed. Rachel has become "the mother of the nation" and, despite or because of her tragic end, a figure of comfort and of hope.

A view through the window of the public bus to Rachel's Tomb as it takes a circuitous (and fascinating) route through Jerusalem's ultra-Orthodox neighborhood of Meah She'arim.

Rachel shares this title with her sister/co-wife Leah, and both are invoked in the blessing of the union of Boaz and Ruth (Ruth 4:11). Jeremiah visualizes Rachel weeping for the children of Israel, who trudged into exile within sight of her tomb (Jeremiah 31:15). Matthew quotes Jeremiah to reveal Rachel weeping for actual children—those of Bethlehem who were murdered by Herod the Great.

One legend about Rachel's Tomb states that Jacob buried Rachel near Bethlehem because he foresaw how Rachel would call forth God's mercy on the exiles passing by Bethlehem after the Babylonian conquest.[1] Legend also says that of all the Israelite leaders who came before

---

1 Genesis Rabbah 82:10.

Moses Montefiore. Mother Rachel would have approved of the great support he gave to the first Jews who came back to the land. A picture of that building, a symbol of the return, could be found in Jewish homes throughout the world in those days.

God pleading to restore Israel, only Rachel, a selfless and a modest woman, obtained God's promise to do so. "You will be rewarded for your work," says Jeremiah 31:16, prophesying that restoration. What was that "work"? Perhaps, in the spirit of the sages' interpretation of "modesty," overcoming her jealousy of Leah.[2]

By the Middle Ages, Rachel's Tomb was a well-established place of pilgrimage. Travelers who stopped there say they saw eleven stones, laid by each of the eleven eldest sons of Jacob at Rachel's death, and a large stone laid by Jacob. Over the years, a dome was built over the tomb, as drawings by numerous pilgrims attest.

In 1483, a Christian visitor from Mainz, Germany was the first to describe women praying here and collecting stones to take home that they believed would ease their labor. Muslim women also came to sanctify the Tomb of Rachel; a Muslim cemetery still surrounds the site.

In 1865 the ancient structure was renovated with funds provided by the British-Jewish philanthropist Sir

Today, women especially sense that God hears their petition when they come to Rachel's Tomb. The New Moon, the beginning of the Hebrew month, which has become a special women's prayer time, is a common occasion to make the pilgrimage here. The Tomb of Rachel is now on the seam between Palestinian- and Israeli-controlled areas, and the little Montefiore building with the tomb inside no longer sees the light of day. Rather, it is accessed by a tunnel to protect visitors in case of unrest. Even so, the hundreds of people who flock here daily prove that Rachel's spirit can never be locked away.

Above: *These prayer books, psalters, and other devotional works found in niches near the tomb show the awaiting of the faithful and their hasty return to the bus back to Jerusalem.*

2 Babylonian Talmud, Megillah 13a–b.

57

The bus station is an eclectic blend of specialty shops and aromatic restaurants. The center court is lined end-to-end in colorful displays of merchandise for the number of tourists who will, at the appropriate time, use the bus station for the purpose for which it was designed. We have passed security, made inquiries and purchases, and dined on sandwiches and cappuccinos. We are ready now for what we have come to do.

We take a seat on one of the inside benches of the top floor and wait in the semi-darkness for our bus. Next to me is a young Jewish woman of such striking beauty that I find myself captivated. Like me and the many others who will take the 1:15 to Rachel's Tomb, she waits in quiet anticipation. Unlike me, she has a more desperate purpose: to pray near the tomb of Israel's mother.

The bus stops on congested streets, adding passengers whose dress is becoming familiar. Long-bearded men dressed in black, heads covered in dark hats and ringlets of hair over sideburns. Women wearing simple dresses cut from dreary fabric, heads covered by pretty scarves. Every inch of Jerusalem's Meah She'arim, an Orthodox Jewish settlement founded in 1874, bursts with modern antiquity.

Eventually Jerusalem's cityscape turns rural. We stop at a checkpoint where a heavily armed soldier steps on the bus. The bus chugs forward again until we pass through a security gate and then slip between high walls of concrete.

I have not been this safe since I was in my mother's womb.

And then the bus stops, the door swings open, and our guard steps out. He is met by others who hurry us inside the building. Just beyond the entryway is a fountain where the Orthodox wash their hands in preparation. We pause, then we move down a wide hall; shuffling feet and the chanting of men heard from places I cannot enter echo in a cool passageway of lingering cigarette smoke.

Seconds later we step down to the women's outer chamber. It is remarkably cold—the ancient stones beneath my feet are cracked and stained with time—and scattered with psalm booklets. Arched bookshelves carved into walls hold prayer books; they lay in a jumble on one, precisely aligned in another. They are much like the prayers, coming from the inner room where a velvet-draped structure protects the one large rock and eleven small rocks believed to have been placed over Rachel's grave by Jacob and his eleven eldest sons.

I slip inside, allowing my fingertips to brush across the mezuzah as I enter. I watch. I listen. I pray.

But not as these women pray. They both humbly petition and boldly beg God for that which brought them here.

In spite of the distance.

In spite of the danger.

The air leaves my lungs with such velocity, I can hardly breathe. *What price these people pay to pray. You are that important to them. Drawing near to you—come what may—is vital to life itself.*

But is it for me? Would I risk my life just to pray? Would it be—could it be—that essential to my relationship with God? And if not, why not?

Right page: *A beautiful young woman stands in fervent prayer and seems transformed by her moments with the Matriarch.*

The Philistines gathered their armies for war . . . . Saul and the Israelites gathered in the Valley of Elah and camped there and took their positions to fight the Philistines. The Philistines controlled one hill while the Israelites controlled another. The valley was between them. The Philistines had a champion fighter from Gath named Goliath. He was about nine feet, four inches tall.

David said to Saul, "Don't let anyone be discouraged. I, your servant, will go and fight this Philistine!" Saul answered, "You can't go out against this Philistine and fight him. You're only a boy. Goliath has been a warrior since he was a young man." But David said to Saul, "I, your servant, have been keeping my father's sheep. When a lion or bear came and took a sheep from the flock, I would chase it. I would attack it and save the sheep from its mouth. When it attacked me, I caught it by its fur and hit it and killed it. I, your servant, have killed both a lion and a bear! This uncircumcised Philistine will be like them, because he has spoken against the armies of the living God. The LORD who saved me from a lion and a bear will save me from this Philistine." Saul said to David, "Go, and may the LORD be with you." Saul put his own clothes on David. He put a bronze helmet on his head and dressed him in armor. David put on Saul's sword and tried to walk around, but he was not used to all the armor Saul had put on him. He said to Saul, "I can't go in this, because I'm not used to it." Then David took it all off.

He took his stick in his hand and chose five smooth stones from a stream. He put them in his shepherd's bag and grabbed his sling. Then he went to meet the Philistine. At the same time, the Philistine was coming closer to David. The man who held his shield walked in front of him. When Goliath looked at David and saw that he was only a boy, tanned and handsome, he looked down on David with disgust. He said, "Do you think I am a dog, that you come at me with a stick?" He used his gods' names to curse David. He said to David, "Come here. I'll feed your body to the birds of the air and the wild animals!" But David said to him, "You come to me using a sword and two spears. But I come to you in the name of the LORD All-Powerful, the God of the armies of Israel! You have spoken against him. Today the LORD will hand you over to me, and I'll kill you and cut off your head. Today I'll feed the bodies of the Philistine soldiers to the

Valley of Elah

Framed by a blossoming almond branch, a view of the Elah Valley from Tel Azeka, where David fought Goliath.

birds of the air and the wild animals. Then all the world will know there is a God in Israel! Everyone gathered here will know the LORD does not need swords or spears to save people. The battle belongs to him, and he will hand you over to us."

As Goliath came near to attack him, David ran quickly to meet him. He took a stone from his bag, put it into his sling, and slung it. The stone hit the Philistine and went deep into his forehead, and Goliath fell facedown on the ground. So David defeated the Philistine with only a sling and a stone. He hit him and killed him. He did not even have a sword in his hand. Then David ran and stood beside him. He took Goliath's sword out of its holder and killed him by cutting off his head.

When Saul saw David go out to meet Goliath, Saul asked Abner, commander of the army, "Abner, who is that young man's father?" Abner answered, "As surely as you live, my king, I don't know." The king said, "Find out whose son he is." When David came back from killing Goliath, Abner brought him to Saul. David was still holding Goliath's head. Saul asked him, "Young man, who is your father?" David answered, "I am the son of your servant Jesse of Bethlehem."

Excerpted from 1 Samuel 17

In the Elah Valley you don't have to close your eyes to imagine the Bible coming to life; you have to open them. Part of the frontier between Judah and the Mediterranean coast in antiquity, Elah was literally the "wild west" and saw more drama than any Hollywood western could ever dream of. Joshua 10:40 describes this region where the Judean mountains give way to the coastal plain as "western hills." Plain words, these, but seemingly sufficient for this region where the Judean mountains peter out. But in terms of strategy and tactics, for the Israelites—and every other army that fought until Israel's modern-day struggles—it was everything.

The home of Samson is not far from here, as is Beth Shemesh, from where messengers quickly ran to Azekah with the joyous news that the Ark of the Lord had returned to their town from Philistine captivity.

Northwest of here, the Ajalon Valley is probably better known than Elah because there the moon refused to set and the sun stood still (Joshua 10:12). The Canaanites were blinded as they attempted to scramble up the mountains to battle against the Israelites. But it was at

The scrubby terebinth trees (Elah in Hebrew) that gave this valley its name cling to the hills above the streambed.

Tel Azekah, overlooking the Elah Valley, where on that same battle-weary day, God delivered the *coup de grâce* to the Canaanite army: a hailstorm caught them as they fled

Azekah saw hard days, too. Centuries after Joshua's victory, Azekah and the neighboring city of Lachish were the last bastions against the Babylonian onslaught that turned Solomon's Temple into rubble and sent Jerusalem into exile (Jeremiah 34:7). An ancient Hebrew message written on a broken shard found at Lachish reads, "We can no longer see the signal fires of Azekah," and may be poignant testimony to those sad days.

The moon gleamed long and bright in Ajalon, but here in the Elah Valley, the courageous spirit of David shone just as brightly as he faced Goliath, the overgrown champion of the Philistines. And the land itself still tells that tale.

The Philistines penetrated the land from the west. At the same time, the Israelites were coming into the land from the east. And so they would meet at the Valley

avid and Goliath's lowland battlefield may not have monumental ruins or famed ancient cities, but the very topography—the valley where the Israelites and the Philistines arrayed, the stream where David picked up his stones—help tell the ancient tale. Thus, this region, a relatively undeveloped area of Israel, is one of those considered a "heritage complex," by the initiators of Israel's Open Spaces Project. In such places (among others, the area of the Samson stories in Israel's lowlands around Beth Shemesh and the Jezreel Valley, where many biblical battles took place), local and national government as well as residents will harness their energies in the coming years to ensure its preservation as a precious remnant of biblical history.

Scripture has been inscribed in pillars for pilgrims to read as they ascend Azekah.

of Elah, a frontier between the two nations warring over land that belongs to God.

At Azekah we can hear the clanking of the two armies moving into position, between the cities of Azekah and Socoh. *The Philistines controlled one hill while the Israelites controlled another. The valley was between them* (1 Samuel 17:3). We clamber down the rocky slopes of Tel Azekah and make for the Elah Stream, where there are still plenty of "smooth stones" (1 Samuel 17:40) for the taking, rounded as they tumbled through a rain-swollen winter stream from Bethlehem's heights.

Socoh peers out from behind the hills; beyond it is the city of David—Bethlehem—which he left to bring victory to his people, armed with the only weapons he needed—his shepherd's skill and the help of God.

It is such a part of the landscape, one hardly notices it. Driving winding roads to leave Jerusalem, it is no more than a verdant valley with sloping hills on either side. A narrow, dried-up brook snaking through it is no more impressive than the countless flat, white stones lining its bed and banks. Yet our car is forced to slow to a stop; a bottleneck of traffic has deposited those who would come to see and take from the Valley of Elah.

We choose not to join them, but instead climb a nearly hidden pathway up the hilltop of Azekah. It is so steep; I wheeze rather than breathe. Along the way, we stop to read Scripture verses etched into square stone pillars, erected for the sake of remembrance.

Reaching the top, we pause to catch our breath, then gasp again in wonder at the expansive valley below. Left to right, front to back, it seems to reach to forever.

Springtime, when the almond trees blossom in the Holy Land, is the best time to consider Jeremiah 1:11–12: "The Lord spoke his word to me, saying: 'Jeremiah, what do you see?' I answered, 'I see a stick of almond wood.' The Lord said to me, 'You have seen correctly, because I am watching to make sure my words come true.' What is the connection between almonds and watching? In Hebrew, both words come from the root word for "watch." What better place to consider God's protective power than at the Elah Valley, where David defeated Goliath!

Peering through branches of almond blossoms, I imagine the young boy David coming from the opposite side of the valley. He is dressed in a shepherd's tunic, his sandaled feet thump against thick grass, and his staff pierces the ground before him. He seems nonplussed at first—sling hanging loosely from his fist—his goal only to gather five smooth stones from the brook. Kneeling, he chooses them one at a time, running his fingers over them as though they are fine gems.

And then he stands.

There is a rattling in the camp. Heavy metal jangles as it moves toward the one who has already won the battle because he has enough faith to face the enemy. Seeing the boy's youth and good looks, the giant spews curses. But he cannot rattle the boy, a shepherd who seems ready for nothing more than a game.

When I stand still in this spot, I can hear the laughter of these Philistines. *Go ahead*, I think. *The lad already knows the outcome of this fight.*

There is a wrinkle in time now. The clanking of armor, the *whoosh-whoosh-whoosh* of a skilled sling whipping through the air, the rowdiness of one camp, the noisy gasp of another, the smack of stone striking flesh, and the thunder of earth as Goliath crumples to his death.

The shepherd—who must have looked so petite against the greatness of this land—has slain his giant.

I shiver, though the weather is warm. It's not the temperature that has chilled me to the bone. It's my lack of faith, standing in the presence of my own giants. It's easy, I decide, to fight them with bravado when in my own camp. But do I dare step out into the valley? Have I practiced with sling and stone enough while in valleys of pleasure to know what I'm doing in valleys of war? Have I mastered the turn of the wrist, the height of the arm? Do I know just when to let go?

Do I even know how?

Left: The flowering of prophecy: Jeremiah taught us how even the blossoming of the almond recalls God's watchfulness over us

Left page: A modern shepherd boy chases his flock along a road near the Valley of Elah in the footsteps of the shepherd, David.

That night, some shepherds were in the fields nearby watching their sheep. Then an angel of the Lord stood before them. The glory of the Lord was shining around them, and they became very frightened. The angel said to them, "Do not be afraid. I am bringing you good news that will be a great joy to all the people. Today your Savior was born in the town of David. He is Christ, the Lord. This is how you will know him: You will find a baby wrapped in pieces of cloth and lying in a feeding box." Then a very large group of angels from heaven joined the first angel, praising God and saying: "Give glory to God in heaven, and on earth let there be peace among the people who please God." When the angels left them and went back to heaven, the shepherds said to each other, "Let's go to Bethlehem. Let's see this thing that has happened which the Lord has told us about." So the shepherds went quickly and found Mary and Joseph and the baby, who was lying in a feeding box. When they had seen him, they told what the angels had said about this child. Everyone was amazed at what the shepherds said to them. But Mary treasured these things and continued to think about them. Then the shepherds went back to their sheep, praising God and thanking him for everything they had seen and heard. It had been just as the angel had told them.

Luke 2:8–20

Shepherds' Fields

A shepherd leads his sheep across the rocky terrain on the fringe of the Judean Desert outside of Bethlehem, where there is just enough sustenance to nourish the flock.

The three locations where Shepherds' Fields have been marked are within walking distance of one another, in the village of Beit Sahour, east of Bethlehem. Once this was all open land. Now you can hardly see the fields because houses have gone up around them over the years, cutting them off from each other. On each patch of once-open field rises a church—three different sects laying claim to the "authentic" site where the angels proclaimed the birth of Jesus to shepherds on the watch.

At Ramat Rachel, "the height of Rachel," not far from Rachel's Tomb on the southern edge of Jerusalem, the ruins of a church mark the site where tradition says Mary rested on her way to Bethlehem. There you can see what is left of the Shepherds' Fields and get acquainted with a special region known as "the frontier of the desert." Like the foothills on the western slopes that divide these mountains of Judah from the coastal plain, this area is very strategic. The band of grain fields beyond the last houses of Beit Sahour, greening at the end of winter and golden by Pentecost, is the outer fringe of the settled land. The land is rocky, and not as giving as the terraced hills higher to the west, but farmers still raise grain here, watered by the grace of heaven—the winter rains. Beyond it lies the wilderness, where shepherds still pasture their flocks. Further east lie the "desolate waste" (Jeremiah 32:43 NIV) and the depths of the Dead Sea rift. Then the land rises once again toward the mountains of Moab—homeland of Ruth.

What's in a name? In the case of Beit Sahour and Bethlehem—understanding. *Beit Sahour* means "house of stone," and *Bethlehem* means "house of bread."

As Ruth walked up toward the House of Bread, she would have passed among the harvesters (Ruth 1:22) in what became the Shepherds' Fields. In accordance with ancient Jewish law (Leviticus 19:9), Ruth, the sole support of her little household, was allowed to glean at the sides of the field (Ruth 2:3). The word for "sides" *(peyot)* of the field in Hebrew is the same as the word for the "sides" of the head, or side-curls required of the Israelites (Leviticus 19:27) and still worn by Orthodox men. Jewish sages determined that the otherwise inexplicable reason for God's interest in hairstyling was

Shepherds' Fields, traditionally the same place as the "Fields of Boaz" where Ruth harvested grain, is within sight of the road Ruth could have taken as she headed form Moab toward Bethlehem with Naomi. Many would have plied this road leading from points east to the mountains of Judah, shepherds and merchants, the high-born and the low. This is a good place to consider that Ruth, a brave woman from a foreign land who threw her lot in with Naomi's people, shared an important trait not only with the simple shepherds of the Nativity Story, but also with the high-born Magi (Matt. 2:1-2). sent by Herod on a nefarious duty. Both "followed their star," searching until they found their everlasting treasure.

The buildings of Bethlehem, the "house of bread" stretching eastward to Beit Sahour, the "house of stone" on the edge of the Judean Desert, that drops away to the Dead Sea Valley, beyond which rise the Mountains of Moab.

that in using the same Hebrew word for "sides" in both cases, men would never forget the poor.

Shepherds' Fields is also known as the Fields of Boaz because, according to tradition, the great-grandfather of David owned this land. Centuries later, it was here that the shepherds, who by custom could bring their flocks in to feed on what was left after the harvest, were the first to receive the news of the Nativity (Luke 2:8). Thus, Ruth and the shepherds both came from the House of Stone to the House of Bread, finding sustenance in the House of Stone and their future in the House of Bread.

little town...
No longer so little as the carol goes.
How still...

No longer still, no more filled with the tranquility the hymn implies.

And yet, in Shepherds' Fields the flocks continue to graze as their masters carry on in a time-etched tradition.

We stand on the overlook of Ramat Rachel, my Jewish friend and I, and stare in stony silence at the bustling lush landscape before us. *House of Stone . . . House of Bread.* It is not safe for her to enter the birthplace of Jesus, himself a Jewish babe born of a Jewish girl who made a whispered claim of deity over her son.

Were she alive today—this Mary of Nazareth—she would, no doubt, stop along the way and pray near her mother Rachel, asking that God watch over her as she gave birth. But she would not be able to enter into the gates of the birthplace of her father, David, without fear.

I wonder, as I look across the ancient and the modern, how my friend is feeling at this moment. Is it close to how I feel? Can our hearts be so joined, in spite of her heritage and in spite of mine?

I wonder.

The setting sun casts pink shadows across her already sun-kissed face and, as a gentle breeze sighs from the west, I look toward its origin and marvel at the Hills of Moab, warm as croissants fresh from an oven. I close my eyes and open them again, focusing on the haze above the crests, looking for the two women—the Gentile Ruth and the Israelite Naomi—who made their way over them. Did Ruth—as I am now—pause long enough to look at the fields where shepherds watched their flocks and harvesters gathered their grain? Did she contemplate what fate might befall her there? Or did she follow her beloved Naomi in a faith I can only hope to one day grasp?

Slowly . . . slowly . . . I turn my head. My eyes come to rest on the bell tower of the Church of the Nativity, the place commemorating the birth of Jesus, a child born of Ruth's lineage.

Could she have known? Begun to have known?

Could she have imagined that—one day—she could enter, but Naomi *could not?*

"I cannot safely go into Bethlehem." My friend interrupts my musing. "But I *can* get someone to take you in."

I feel a sadness rising up from deep inside me. Tears burn my eyes; I refuse to hold them back. As they trail down my cheeks, I turn to her and say, "Don't ask that of me . . . where you go, I go. Where

ut Ruth said, "Don't beg me to leave you or to stop following you. Where you go, I will go. Where you live, I will live. Your people will be my people, and your God will be my God. And where you die, I will die, and there I will be buried. I ask the Lord to punish me terribly if I do not keep this promise: Not even death will separate us." So Naomi and Ruth went on until they came to the town of Bethlehem.

Excerpted Ruth 1

you lodge, I lodge. Your people are my people. Your God, my God."

In unison we look to our city—birthplace of the shepherd David, birthplace of the Great Shepherd Jesus. But our thoughts move on, past the inner strife, to the place where shepherds watch and sheep graze.

And a harvest waits to be gathered.

The ripening grain holds the promise of spring. For Ruth the Moabite, gleaning in the fields of Bethlehem, it meant the promise of new life.

At that time, Augustus Caesar sent an order that all people in the countries under Roman rule must list their names in a register. This was the first registration; it was taken while Quirinius was governor of Syria. And all went to their own towns to be registered. So Joseph left Nazareth, a town in Galilee, and went to the town of Bethlehem in Judea, known as the town of David. Joseph went there because he was from the family of David. Joseph registered with Mary, to whom he was engaged and who was now pregnant. While they were in Bethlehem, the time came for Mary to have the baby, and she gave birth to her first son. Because there were no rooms left in the inn, she wrapped the baby with pieces of cloth and laid him in a feeding trough.

Luke 2:1–7

Church of the Nativity

For some 1,500 years, the vast colonnaded sanctuary of the Church of the Nativity has been leading worshippers to the traditional birthplace of Jesus.

he only visible entrance to "the earth's most sacred spot," as this place was deemed by Christian scholar Jerome more than 1,600 years ago, seems like a mouse hole in contrast to its massive stone ramparts. Ducking through it, you enter a dimension where sacred memory is more powerful than any force on earth.

The mingled aromas of incense and kerosene greet you as you as you cross into the cavernous, stone-paved sanctuary. Sunlight streaming in from high windows unsuccessfully gives chase to the shadows cast by rows of gigantic columns. Little knots of tourists listen raptly to their guides. Peering through a trap door at a magnificent bit of mosaic flooring, they hear it is a remnant of the glory days of Constantine and Justinian, the Christian builder-kings. They gather around a cistern, where they hear that the star that led the Magi here fell in and fizzled out. They even see where the Muslim conqueror Omar said his prayers in the seventh century.

Luke tells us that the baby Jesus was "laid in a manger"—a feeding trough. Thus the "nativity scene" that emerged over the centuries has Joseph, Mary, and the newborn Jesus surrounded by barn animals. In Jesus' day, mangers for farm animals were placed in the

caves of the type that pock these Judean hills. Jerome was the first to point out that a cave was the birthplace of Jesus. It was surrounded by a grove, and by the time of Emperor Hadrian, Christians could only watch from afar as pagan women wept over the summer-solstice death of Tammuz, who by Hadrian's day was called Adonis. Then. on May 31, 329, King Constantine's mother. Queen Helene. dedicated the first Christian house of worship here. Less than a century later Justinian enlarged the church, and then in 614 the Persians invaded. Legend says they thought a mural of the Magi depicted Persian sages, and spared the church the destruction inflicted at other Christian holy sites. Over the years the church mushroomed into a multi-leveled labyrinth of chambers and caverns, each with its own sacred tradition: here—the burial place of the Innocents; there—St. Jerome's study. All surrounded by the gigantic walls that kept every invader at bay.

Worn stone steps now lead into the cave of the Nativity. Every piece of wall was eventually covered with paintings, mosaics, tapestries and silver-studded icons of various Christian sects and their patrons—the crowned

Left page: *Adorned and adored over the centuries, hardly a remnant of the natural walls of the Cave of the Nativity can be seen today. At center, the Greek Orthodox site of the nativity, flanked by the steps leading up to the sanctuary. At right, the Roman Catholic shrine.*

The Church of the Nativity, in which control is shared by many Christian sects, was, ironically, where the first sparks of the Crimean War were ignited, over the fate of a silver star that marked the place of Jesus' birth. The star was removed by persons unknown around 1845. Symbolizing control not only of the sacred site, but strategic influence in the Holy Land, the star's theft quickly became a cause celebre. The Greek and Armenian Orthodox, who claimed ownership, accused the Roman Catholic Franciscans of the deed, and vice-versa. The French and other Catholic powers supported the Franciscans; the Russians backed the Greek Orthodox. The ruling Turks insisted that the star be returned but repulsed foreign interference, leading in 1853 to the outbreak of hostilities between Russia and Europe's Catholic nations, which ended with Russia's defeat in 1856.

heads of Europe who supported the churches to protect their stake in this strategic land.

The grotto walls, too, are covered with stiff asbestos wall hangings to guard against fires from pilgrims' candles. The birthplace of Jesus is marked by a silver star, the replacement of one whose mysterious disappearance in 1847 led Europe to battle against the Russians in the Crimean War.

As you emerge from the Church of the Nativity, your head swirls with hundreds of historical details. Amazingly, they do not fade, but come together in recognition of how an ancient fortress of faith came into being and endures.

For many years, my eyes—and therefore my heart—have beheld a picture of a hay-filled, barn-type, three-sided structure. Inside are a young woman—looking quite resplendent after hours spent in the throes of labor and delivery—and an awe-inspired man peering down on a perfectly formed Caucasian baby. From the left (or sometimes the right) comes a trio of men draped in thick, oversized robes, pulling their camels behind them. From the right (or sometimes the left) is a cluster of shepherds and, in particular, one boy holding a small drum. All around are farm animals, and, above everything, an angel perches, seemingly on air.

If I didn't know the scene was not *based* on truth, I would think it no more than a fairy tale. But, based on truth is all it can be. Mary and Joseph were a poor Jewish couple who—no doubt—would have looked as though they'd just spent hours in emotional panic and physical distress. The precious baby would have had the olive complexion of a Hebrew child. Whether he slept peacefully or squirmed against the chill of life is anyone's guess.

The Bible tells us that it was not an angel but a host of them that filled the sky that evening. The true Nativity story tells us of shepherds but never of a drummer boy. It could have been two years or more before the caravan of magi arrived. The Bible never mentions a cave, though it certainly falls within reason.

But there are many who believe Jesus, named Yeshua by his parents, was born during the feast known as Sukkot, or The Feast of Tabernacles (Booths). Their belief is that he may have been born in any of the number of temporary booths dotting Bethlehem's landscape as a part of the celebration. Others believe that Mary and Joseph, taken in by family in Bethlehem, brought their child into the world in the "first floor" of a home where farm animals were often kept at night.

Whether cave or booth or first-floor accommodations, there would have been neither rows of impressive Corinthian columns surrounding them nor marble flooring etched in gold upon which Mary would position herself. There would have been neither draperies of rich fabrics nor walls dripping with icons.

Unlike many who have come and who will come in the future, I choose not to enter or even to try to enter. I stand, instead, on a hilltop and look down on the place that is no longer a simple village but a sprawling city. I imagine that Mary, a young girl who pondered much in her heart, might blush at such a notion of people flocking to see this public display of her very private moment.

And then, across rocky terrain and years of religious honor, I see her smile. I wink at her, and she nods at me. She understands, I think, that I have chosen to allow her son to be born in my heart.

Any other place is just geography.

isitors have been inspired by birthplace of Jesus for generations. Phillips Brooks (1835–1903), an Episcopal rector from Philadelphia, wrote the words to one of the most gentle and beloved hymns after a visit to the Holy Land in 1865. Unable to forget what he experienced on the streets of Bethlehem, he penned the words that today almost every child knows by heart.

O Little Town of Bethlehem

O little town of Bethlehem
How still we see thee lie
Above thy deep and dreamless sleep
The silent stars go by
Yet in thy dark streets shineth
The everlasting light
The hopes and fears of all the years
Are met in thee tonight

From the Mountains to the Sea

When Jabin king of Hazor heard about all that had happened, he sent messages to Jobab king of Madon, to the king of Shimron, and to the king of Acshaph. He sent messages to the kings in the northern mountains and also to the kings in the Jordan Valley south of Lake Galilee and in the western hills. He sent a message to the king of Naphoth Dor in the west and to the kings of the Canaanites in the east and in the west. He sent messages to the Amorites, Hittites, Perizzites, and Jebusites in the mountains. Jabin also sent one to the Hivites, who lived below Mount Hermon in the area of Mizpah. So the armies of all these kings came together with their horses and chariots. There were as many soldiers as grains of sand on the seashore. All of these kings met together at the waters of Merom, joined their armies together into one camp, and made plans to fight against the Israelites. Then the Lord said to Joshua, "Don't be afraid of them, because at this time tomorrow I will give them to you. You will cripple their horses and burn all their chariots." So Joshua and his whole army surprised the enemy by attacking them at the waters of Merom. The Lord handed them over to Israel. They chased them to Greater Sidon, Misrephoth Maim, and the Valley of Mizpah in the east. Israel fought until none of the enemy was left alive. Joshua did what the Lord said to do; he crippled their horses and burned their chariots.

Then Joshua went back and captured the city of Hazor and killed its king. (Hazor had been the leader of all the kingdoms that fought against Israel.) Israel killed everyone in Hazor, completely destroying them; no one was left alive. Then they burned Hazor itself. Joshua captured all of these cities, killed all of their kings, and completely destroyed everything in these cities. He did this just as Moses, the servant of the Lord, had commanded. But the Israelites did not burn any cities that were built on their mounds, except Hazor; only that city was burned by Joshua.

Joshua 11:1–13

Tel Hazor

*These rows of columns supported the roof of a large public
building from the Israelite period at Hazor.*

ven in ruin, the mighty city of Hazor still casts its shadow across the road—now a modern highway—and across the millennia. Traders and armies once traveled this road—north to Babylon and Damascus; west to Phoenicia, the Great Sea, and beyond to Cyprus, Crete, and Greece; and south to Egypt. Constant building and destruction have raised stratum upon stratum of civilization here, 120 feet above the valley floor, a huge layer-cake of history into which the archaeologists have sliced to bring us the past on a silver platter.

Some five thousand years have passed since people first founded their homes at Hazor in the fertile land of the Hula Valley and within comfortable distance of a spring. By around the eighteenth century BC, Hazor had a population of fifteen thousand and was connected to all the great cities of the day. Documents found at Mari on the Euphrates and el-Amarna in Egypt tell of royal courts, ambassadors, richly laden commercial caravans, musicians, and singers. No wonder the Bible would call Hazor "the head of all these kingdoms" (Joshua 11:10 NIV). Biblical history sings out loud and clear from these documents. They mention a king who probably bequeathed his dynastic name *Ibni*—Jabin—to a descendant who fought Joshua and another who doomed his general, Sisera, to do battle against the army of Deborah and Barak.

No monarch worth his salt could afford to ignore Hazor. And so the Bible says Solomon, who fortified other strategic cities such as Megiddo and Gezer, stamped his imprint on Hazor too. The remnants of powerful walls and gates testify to that imprint. Its complex water system and storehouses, built during the Israelite rule, attest to a city of wealth and organization.

Hazor's ceremonial palace, built by the Canaanite kings who ruled here in the fourteenth and thirteenth centuries BC, is the jewel in its crown. The lower parts of its mud-brick walls were covered with black basalt slabs, the upper portions with magnificent cedar wood paneling. Inscribed clay tablets, figurines, and jewelry were all unearthed in its ruins. Sometime in the thirteenth century BC, a great fire engulfed the

Above: *A fruit-bearing mandrake plant (Gen. 30: 14) thrives in a garden patch on Tel Hazor.*

Left page: *Warriors of bygone days are remembered in this statue guarding the ruins of Hazor.*

palace. You can still see—still touch—the sooty remains some are tempted to ascribe to the day Joshua *burned Hazor with fire.*

Joshua's strategy, honed in his earlier battles for Judah, was stunningly simple and suited to a generation who had no other way of combating the ancient and deadly version of the armored personnel carrier first mentioned in the battle of Hazor—the war chariot. The Canaanite armies converged at a central crossroads of the Hula Valley, the Waters of Merom, which unfortunately for them was also a narrow gorge. Joshua waited and surprised the enemy. Their chariots were no good to them there; Joshua's forces "fell upon them" in a strike that serves as a fine example of how the few against the many can win the day.

In 2005, Tel Hazor was inscribed as a World Heritage Site by the United Nations Educational, Scientific and Cultural Organization (UNESCO). According to the criteria for inscription, because of Tel Hazor's location on the ancient Near Eastern trade highway it fostered "an interchange of human values...manifest in building styles that merged Egyptian, Syrian and Aegean influence to create a distinctive local style." It is also considered a manifestation of the creativity of its builders and exerted "a powerful influence on later history through the biblical narrative."*

*UNESCO inscription criteria

he canopy of sky—clear blue and cloudless— arches over its earth as the sun rises lazily over the sloping hillsides, groomed with rich green grass and rainbows of wildflowers. All of nature stretches and groans in the wake of morning, then lifts praise to its Creator. From the north, Mount Hermon stands like a grandfather watching over his offspring, proudly stroking his thick white beard.

I have truly returned home. This is the place of beginnings for me; the place where God spoke into my life with a single sentence from a gentle man: "You are touching the Bible."

The fire-blackened remains of a palace wall at Hazor, where Eva Marie "fell into the Bible" for the first time.

The gates of Hazor open wide, embracing us with a dignity neither destruction nor time can ruin. As I step between them, I imagine the number of those who have entered throughout the millennia—those who would rule the world and those who only wanted to be ruled by God.

It is not the stones and relics that draw my attention. It's not the obvious landscape. Hazor had been the leader of all these kingdoms—with its roads leading to and through it. Nor is it the evidence of the Ages, the rise of one king and then another and another, nor is it the tangible proof of lifetimes brought to their knees.

It is the verdant rolling near the ancient, rising in places, dipping to level ground in others. It is the image. Within this place I see a fierce slave-turned-warrior; I see Joshua, leader of Israel's army. Servant of Moses,

A tower the Israelites built against Assyrian attack (2 Kings 15:29) reminds us that these defenses fell against Assyrian King Tiglath-Pileser.

servant of the Most High, Joshua has pushed back his fears and—trusting God—has crossed the Jordan with a nation behind him, defeated the fortified city of Jericho, and watched as its impenetrable walls crumbled. He has witnessed God's fury over Achan's disobedience, built an altar and renewed a covenant with the Almighty, then fought in awe as Nature obeyed her Master, holding the sun in place and hurling hailstones upon his enemies.

The central Canaanite cities had bowed to his authority, the southern followed suit, and finally the northern kings, led by Jabin of Hazor, have fallen. And now, with sheer determination etched across his face, he turns back and commands his ragged troops, "As we did before God in Jericho, burn her to the ground!"

The words echo between the hills; they swirl around these ruins of the great Hazor, nearly lost to time and history. They rise up in my heart, and my entire body shivers in anticipation of what I know is near the bottom of this tel.

It is the soot, some say, from Joshua's fire.

I am given special permission to touch it, to feel its velvet beneath my fingertips. To see with my eyes the evidence of God's power in a man—in his soul—that is determined to trust the word and direction of *El Shaddai*.

Be strong and courageous, he said to Joshua.

"Be strong and courageous," he now says to me. I look up again to the hills and whisper, "I will obey. I will obey."

The angel of the LORD appeared to Gideon and said, "The LORD is with you, mighty warrior!"

Early in the morning Jerub-Baal (also called Gideon) and all his men set up their camp at the spring of Harod. The Midianites were camped north of them in the valley at the bottom of the hill called Moreh. Then the LORD said to Gideon, "You have too many men to defeat the Midianites. I don't want the Israelites to brag that they saved themselves. So now, announce to the people, 'Anyone who is afraid may leave Mount Gilead and go back home.'" So twenty-two thousand men returned home, but ten thousand remained. Then the LORD said to Gideon, "There are still too many men. Take the men down to the water, and I will test them for you there. If I say, 'This man will go with you, he will go. But if I say, 'That one will not go with you,' he will not go." So Gideon led the men down to the water. There the LORD said to him, "Separate them into those who drink water by lapping it up like a dog and those who bend down to drink." There were three hundred men who used their hands to bring water to their mouths, lapping it as a dog does. All the rest got down on their knees to drink. Then the LORD said to Gideon, "Using the three hundred men who lapped the water, I will save you and hand Midian over to you. Let all the others go home." So Gideon sent the rest of Israel to their homes. But he kept three hundred men and took the jars and the trumpets of those who left. Now the camp of Midian was in the valley below Gideon.

Gideon divided the three hundred men into three groups. He gave each man a trumpet and an empty jar with a burning torch inside. Gideon told the men, "Watch me and do what I do. When I get to the edge of the camp, do what I do. Surround the enemy camp. When I and everyone with me blow our trumpets, you blow your trumpets, too. Then shout, 'For the LORD and for Gideon!'" So Gideon and the one hundred men with him came to the edge of the enemy camp just after they had changed guards. It was during the middle watch of the night. Then Gideon and his men blew their trumpets and smashed their jars. All three groups of Gideon's men blew their trumpets and smashed their jars. They held the torches in their left hands and the trumpets in their right hands. Then they shouted, "A sword for the LORD and for Gideon!" Each of Gideon's men stayed in his place around the camp, but the Midianites began shouting and running to escape. When Gideon's three hundred men blew their trumpets, the LORD made all the Midianites fight each other with their swords!

Judges 6:12; 7:1–8, 16–22a

Ein Harod

*The spring
of Harod
turns into a
shaded brook.*

he story of Gideon, the unlikely hero of Ein Harod, inspired a modern-day warrior, Major General Orde Charles Wingate, who loved the Bible and the Jewish people and linked his fate to both.

Born in India in 1903 to a Protestant missionary family, Wingate immersed himself in the Bible from a young age. By the time he finished the Royal Military Academy and was posted to Sudan, he was imbued with a sense of spiritual mission. Wingate would have learned the story of Gideon at his parents' feet. His righteous anger would have burned as he pictured the Midianites thundering out of the eastern deserts to plunder the Israelites' harvests and homes (Judges 6:3–6). He may have puzzled over Gideon's series of odd experiments (Judges 6:36–40) to prove to himself that it was God's will he should liberate his people.

When Wingate was assigned as an intelligence officer to Palestine in 1936, he probably came to Ein Harod in the eastern Jezreel Valley. Sitting on the rocks by the spring, now nestled among the manicured lawns and playgrounds of one of Israel's most popular national parks, Wingate would have appreciated how God trimmed the troops to what seemed like a minimum. Before Gideon made his unique last cut, he watched how

the men drank from the spring to observe their vigilance as soldiers (Judges 7:1–6). As a military man, Wingate would have grasped how Gideon led these "few good men" silently up the Hill of Moreh, and then, in the middle of the night, with torches blinding and trumpets blaring, the enemy met its match (Judges 7:19–22).

By the time Wingate came to Palestine, the Jews' return to their homeland—the Zionist Movement—was in full swing, and so was Arab resistance to it. Just as in Gideon's time, by day the farmers worked their fields, and by night the crops would go up in flames, cattle were rustled, and barns were robbed. Wingate, who knew that the lessons of the living Bible still applied and the spirit of Gideon could still be mustered, received reluctant permission from the British authorities to organize the Jewish farmers into night-fighting squads. His work was top-secret; he was known to the Jewish community only by his code name, *Hayedid*, "the friend."

In 1938, Wingate went back to England to recover from an injury. Concerned over his loyalties, Wingate's superiors kept him there. A year later, World War II broke out. After fighting with valor in Ethiopia, East Africa, and India, on March 24, 1944, Wingate crashed into the jungles of India while flying a US B-25 aircraft. Only the distinctive helmet he wore was ever found. Since most of those flying with him were Ameri-

When we first meet Gideon, he is anything but an ordinary hero. In fact, he seems quite the opposite of a hero, hiding his produce and himself in a wine-press as he worked (Judges 6:11), and demanding sign after sign from the angel who appeared before him. But the angel met every test Gideon proposed, and then presented Gideon with one: to tear down the altar to Ba'al set up by his own father together with the people of his village. Earning the nickname "Jerub-Ba'al" (which we might translate very freely: "Ba'al, make my day"), Gideon stood up for the Lord, even against everything he knew and loved. As great as Gideon became, the sages of the Talmud criticized him, denouncing the ephod he made from the spoils of war (Judges 8:24-27). They stated that Gideon, Samson, and Jephthah were among the least worthy of the judges, but concluded that that even such individuals, once they become leaders, can become great (Babylonian Talmud, Rosh Hashanah 25a–b).

cans, all remains were buried together at Arlington National Cemetery.

Wingate was not without his eccentricities, among them depressions he could relieve only by incessantly writing the words "God is good." But it is for his contribution to God's land that he is best remembered. And so if you are ever at Arlington, pause at Section 12, Grave 288[1], and say, "Rest in peace, General Wingate, and thank you."

Left page: The spring of Harod, where Gideon picked his 300 men to fight the Midianites, emerges from this cave.

---

1 Michael Oren, "Orde Wingate: Test of Friendship." *Tchelet* 10 (2001): 27-39 (Hebrew).

 e have entered a children's playground, a far cry from a battlefield or a stage for winnowing soldiers. The lawns are well tended and manicured. There are tables nestled under large shady trees, ideal for family picnics. Along the way I spot hiking trails for those who love a jaunt in the great outdoors, and there is a large swimming pool. Sports equipment dots the landscape as though nothing more significant than child's play ever took place here.

Coarse sand crunches under my feet as we make our way along a winding path with an ever-so-slight incline. We stop long enough to admire the flowers growing from rocky places, then we continue on until we come to Gideon's Cave, a monstrous-looking orifice that opens its jaws, sending water into *Ein Harod,* the Spring of Harod.

Sunlight shimmers on still water and glistens off pebbles lying like gold at the bottom of a treasure chest. I sit upon a large limestone rock, cracked and stained by time. I lean over and put my fingertips to the shallow water, then I watch the rippling effect. I pick up a couple of stones, rolling them around in my hand and, as though they are dice, toss them back.

The ripple becomes larger still.

Sitting up, I take a deep breath and look through the naked limbs of a silk floss tree and beyond a row of olive trees. I study the landscape with its modern additions—fields for play, wires for carrying electricity, fences for keeping in and keeping out, and roads paved for automobiles—to the rise of a hill called Moreh.

There camped the enemy of Gideon. So far away, and yet so close.

What beat might Gideon's heart have made that night? In the eyes of his clan, he was but a weak man threshing wheat while hiding in a winepress; to God, he was a mighty warrior.

But what about to himself?

If you are afraid, God said to Gideon, surely knowing he was scared to the very marrow of his bones, *listen*.

I have moved toward the mountain and am sitting on a low wall of rocks, peering over another wall toward Moreh. I place my arm along the cool and damp stone and lay my chin upon it, gazing over to where Gideon cast aside all fear and conquered the enemy in the name of the Lord.

"Lord," I whisper to him now, "I am afraid. I have my stream to drink from and my valley to cross. I have my battle to fight and my enemy to conquer."

For a moment there is nothing; it is as though all my senses have dried up. Then the olive leaves shimmer in the sun's radiance, and I feel it. It begins as the kiss of the breeze across my skin, and then butterfly wings flutter down my arms. I hear the water from the cave's wall as it kerplunks into the pool and, like a rippling across time, the sound of jars breaking open in the night. Of trumpets blowing and men shouting and an enemy as it turns on itself.

Fear pushes itself from my soul. *Listen . . . listen . . . the Lord is with you, mighty warrior.*

Right: *Ripples of sparkling spring water dance rings around the reflection of the Galilee sun.*

Left page: *Spikey-barked chorisia, a relative of the African baobab tree, keep watch at Gideon's spring. The Hill of Moreh, where Gideon led his soldiers before the battle, rises in the distance.*

Then the LORD God planted a garden in the east, in a place called Eden.

Genesis 2:8a

Then Jeroboam made Shechem in the mountains of Ephraim a very strong city, and he lived there. He also went to the city of Peniel and made it stronger. Jeroboam said to himself, "The kingdom will probably go back to David's family. If the people continue going to the Temple of the LORD in Jerusalem to offer sacrifices, they will want to be ruled again by Rehoboam. Then they will kill me and follow Rehoboam king of Judah." King Jeroboam asked for advice. Then he made two golden calves. "It is too long a journey for you to go to Jerusalem to worship," he said to the people. "Israel, here are your gods who brought you out of Egypt." Jeroboam put one golden calf in the city of Bethel and the other in the city of Dan. This became a very great sin, because the people traveled as far as Dan to worship the calf there. Jeroboam built temples on the places of worship. He also chose priests from all the people, not just from the tribe of Levi.

1 Kings 12:25–31

My sister, my bride, you are like a garden locked up, like a walled-in spring, a closed-up fountain. Your limbs are like an orchard of pomegranates with all the best fruit, filled with flowers and nard, nard and saffron, calamus, and cinnamon, with trees of incense, myrrh, and aloes—all the best spices. You are like a garden fountain—a well of fresh water flowing down from the mountains of Lebanon.

Song of Solomon 4:12–15

Tel Dan

Another face of the Dan, where it eddies into a tranquil pool at the place the locals call "the garden of Eden."

t Dan it may dawn on you that the Holy Land is not the desert of your Sunday school picture books. And why should we have ever thought that? Deuteronomy 8:7 says it best: *a good land—a land with streams and pools of water, with springs flowing in the valleys and hills* (NIV).

The Dan River is rain and snow that has soaked through the great 7,000-foot-high limestone massif of Mount Hermon to the north, emerging cold and powerful from its base. It unites with two other streams to form the Jordan River just a few miles south of here. In fact, the word "Jordan" comes from two Hebrew words—*yored dan*, which means "descending from Dan."

Standing on the banks of this leaping, frothing flow, picture its annual 2.5 million cubic meters surging on to join its sister streams, greening the valley below, and (about twenty-five miles later) pouring into the Sea of Galilee, Israel's greatest lake. Then you can understand why, in modern times, Mount Hermon was deemed "the father of all the water" for this land. But the Psalmist already knew that when he wrote that brotherhood was a precious as "the dew of Hermon" (Psalm 133:3 NIV).

Hikers enjoy the blessings of the water everywhere at Dan, now a lovingly tended nature reserve. The pungent aroma of fig trees fill the air; maidenhair ferns spring from among the rocks; laurel, ash, and even a species of maple tree—all native to northern climates—thrive here. It should not surprise us that the *land the LORD your God cares for* (Deuteronomy 11:12 NIV) has almost every climate zone on the face of the earth, including this northern one.

The river region is strategic; it always has been. Lift your eyes to the hills: towering above the Israeli border outposts with Lebanon is the Nimrod Fortress, a brooding medieval sentinel on the slopes of Hermon, guarding the road to Damascus.

Judges 18:28–29 tells us that the tribe of Dan migrated from the coastal plain to the city that once stood here, called Laish, or Leshem (Joshua 19:47). Over the centuries, Dan grew strong on the river's banks. A shrine went up next to the stream, and its priests probably carried water to pour out in thanksgiving at its altar. Walls sprang up too, and a gate that the archaeologists tell us Father Abraham would have seen when he chased the captors of his nephew Lot *all the way to the town of Dan* (Genesis 14:14). Lovers of Bible lore will note that although the story of

he identification of Tel Dan as the biblical city of the same name is said to have first been made in 1838 by Edward Robinson (1794–1863),* a Connecticut-born theologian who pioneered research into biblical geography. Robinson realized that the Arabic name for the 50-acre mound, Tel el-Qadi, "the judge's mound," harked back to the name "Dan" in the Bible, which means "judge" (Genesis 49:16). The discovery in 1976 of an inscription in Greek and Aramaic "to the god who is in Dan," confirmed the identity of the site as the city of Laish-Dan.

*Professor Avraham Biran, personal communication

The Dan River rushes headlong toward its meeting with the Jordan.

Abraham describes a time when Dan was yet to be, it calls the place Dan; the memory of Laish would dim, but Dan would persevere.

After Solomon died, Jeroboam built a high place here to rival Jerusalem. But then came the Assyrians and with them, the day of Dan's destruction. Today, the water still flows, the hikers drink in the crisp air, and the high place lies in ruin.

y senses—physical and spiritual—have come alive in ways I didn't know possible. My eyes and ears are treated to a wonderland of sights and sounds. My soul is stirred to a peculiar plane, understanding worship at its best and its worst.

Serenity hovers over the waters of the wading pool of the Dan Reserve as delightfully as power reverberates at the places where the melted snow from Hermon charges toward the Jordan. An enchanting sensation comes from the trees soaring toward the azure sky; refreshingly cool air lingers about and kisses my skin. Yet, I am warmed by the sun sending its rays of ethereal light into the shadows and bursting along pathways filled with playful children and strolling lovers.

The desire to run with wild abandon along the trails is cut short as I approach the High Place. The terrain slopes upward as we approach the breadth of steps and stone, but my feet slow for another reason. This was a place where—in spite of its height and beauty, or maybe because of it—God was mocked in worship. My steps are even, and my breathing slows. The very air here is eerily silent. Too silent. Even the sparse trees seem sad. I find no comfort here.

Further to the south are the remains of the Israelite settlement, the Israelite gate, and the towering wall surrounding the city of Dan. Coming from the inside out, I feel as though I am a little mouse in a labyrinth, searching for the little block of cheese at the end.

The massive city walls of Israelite Dan rise in the foreground. Some two millennia later, a nephew of the legendary Saladin first fortified the hill in the background, which became known as Nimrod's Fortress.

Steps leading up to the shrine Jeroboam built at Dan (1 Kings 12:29-31).

And then I find it. Stepping from yesterday to today, I peer around the city's wall. It stretches westward and upward, daring anyone to penetrate the fortress it forms around the settlement. Turning to look behind me, I spot Nimrod's Fortress perched atop a rising hilltop like a crown on a king's head.

A mighty fortress is our God . . . . The song begins from the rhythm of my heart's beat.

I step back around the security of the wall and press myself into one of the corners. Dropping down, I wrap my arms around my knees and, peering up, take in the enormity of protection I feel. My heavenly Father is standing over me. He is rock solid behind me. What,

then, can come against me? What can get to me, tear me down, or break me apart?

What can kill me?

Even here, I am reminded that my life is not without struggle, not without layers of difficulty and conflicts in warfare. Yet there is a fortress, mighty and strong, all around me, keeping me from the weapons I cannot see but most assuredly am aware of.

Now, as peace comes to my soul, I grasp the concept of the fortress in ways I'd not ever considered before. It marks the boundaries of the property—*I am my beloved's, and my beloved is mine*—and makes it a safe haven.

And with that, I can continue onward.

*M*any have tried to report on the things that happened among us. They have written the same things that we learned from others—the people who saw those things from the beginning and served God by telling people his message.

During Elizabeth's sixth month of pregnancy, God sent the angel Gabriel to Nazareth, a town in Galilee, to a virgin. She was engaged to marry a man named Joseph from the family of David. Her name was Mary. The angel came to her and said, "Greetings! The Lord has blessed you and is with you." But Mary was very startled by what the angel said and wondered what this greeting might mean. The angel said to her, "Don't be afraid, Mary; God has shown you his grace. Listen! You will become pregnant and give birth to a son, and you will name him Jesus. He will be great and will be called the Son of the Most High. The Lord God will give him the throne of King David, his ancestor. He will rule over the people of Jacob forever, and his kingdom will never end." Mary said to the angel, "How will this happen since I am a virgin?" The angel said to Mary, "The Holy Spirit will come upon you, and the power of the Most High will cover you. For this reason the baby will be holy and will be called the Son of God. Now Elizabeth, your relative, is also pregnant with a son though she is very old. Everyone thought she could not have a baby, but she has been pregnant for six months. God can do anything!" Mary said, "I am the servant of the Lord. Let this happen to me as you say!" Then the angel went away.

Luke 1:1–2, 26–38

Nazareth

Sunset over Nazareth.

he traditional setting for the event in Luke 1:26–28, known as the Annunciation, was at the spring where Mary had gone to fetch water. This story, attributed to James, the brother of Jesus, in a book that became known as the Apocryphal Gospel of James[1] written in the mid-second century, helps us see Mary as she was in her youth, living with her family in Nazareth. Today the spring, which unites three water sources coming from the mountains behind Nazareth, flows to a well in the crypt of the Greek Orthodox Church of St. Gabriel in Nazareth that is at least eight hundred years old.

But let's picture this scene in the open air, as it was when Mary was here. Once or twice a day, she would lead her donkey to the spring, and then fill her empty jars or goatskin sacks with water. Then she would bring the brimming containers home and pour the water into large, covered jars in her courtyard.

In the arid Holy Land climate, rainless for six months of the year, drawing water was one of the most essential tasks of the household. It was invariably entrusted to the women and young girls, along with baking, spinning, weaving, and tending the flocks and the youngsters.

And Mary would not have been there alone. The well would have been the prime meeting place for the village women, a place to exchange information and advice on virtually everything women everywhere still gather to discuss.

The Church of St. Gabriel is not the only place in Nazareth to mark the Annunciation. The Basilica of the Annunciation, whose dome crowns the city, is a much newer and much bigger church than St. Gabriel's, completed in 1966 by an Israeli construction company. It, too, stands on ancient remains, including caves that once served as storerooms beneath the homes of Nazareth's early inhabitants. When excavations were underway prior to the building of the church, among the finds was a Greek inscription scratched on the base of a column. "Hail Mary" were the words with

---

1 Apocryphal Gospel of James 9:7. In *The Apocryphal New Testament*; M.R. James-Transl. Oxford: Clarendon Press, 1924. Online edition http://www.earlychristianwritings.com/text/infancyjames-mrjames.html.

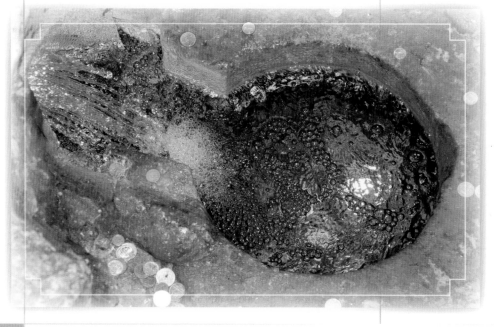

Just up the hill behind Mary's Well, in the Church of St. Gabriel, the faithful cast coins as mementos into the spring where Mary drew water.

which, according to many versions of Luke 1:26, the angel Gabriel greeted Mary. This is the oldest inscription of its kind ever discovered and may have been incised by an early pilgrim to this city, even before the first church was built here in the early fifth century.

The heart of the basilica is the Grotto of the Annunciation, where the tradition of this church says Mary received Gabriel. Near this spot are steps to a baptistery that some scholars believe was used by the Judeo-Christians of Nazareth in the earliest days of the new faith.

On the second story of this complex is the Roman Catholic parish church of Nazareth. This magnificent place of worship is adorned with dozens of mosaics and other artistic depictions of Mary contributed by Christian communities from around the world. From a round balcony near the altar, worshippers and visitors can look down to the Grotto of the Annunciation and maintain eye contact with the ancient remains.

Above: Nazareth's Basilica of the Annunciation is full of symbolism: a "lighthouse" at the top and the repeating triangles representing the Trinity and the first letters of the words Ave Maria—Hail, Mary—which some translations of the gospel say the Angel Gabriel uttered in this spot.

Right: Mary's Well, a landmark in Nazareth for many centuries, in a modern, restored version.

101

Here, they say, from the ornamental mosaics of the upper hall to the cave of the grotto underground, Mary—as a Jew, called Miryam—lived with her family. Here she grew up, she played, and occasionally tussled with her siblings, and she learned to be a wife and a mother by watching Anna, her own mother. Here she learned the Scriptures, the history of her people, and the promise of Messiah.

They say she—as one of seven chosen virgins from David's line—weaved part of the curtain for the Holy of Holies in Jerusalem. But in Nazareth, the Bible tells us, she learned she'd been chosen for an even more impressive role. Here, she shook off fear, took on an even greater amount of faith, and began to live out God's extraordinary plan for her life.

She is all around in this grand hall. Her face shines down upon me from every nation and is represented by every nationality. She is Asian in one place and American in another. But everywhere she is gentle and proud. She is wise and perceptive.

She is a mother.

I am warmed by sunshine. It casts shadows on the public fountain indicating where Mary and her son would have come daily for the water needed to sustain their home and family. As I stand here and watch the playful silhouettes of sun and shade, I wonder about the life she led and how alike or how different it is from mine. She would have worked hard to provide water for her family, where I simply turn on a faucet. But she felt a special call of God on her life and, for that, I can relate.

I am drawn like water.

The doors to the basilica are made of bronze and copper and bear relief carvings depicting the story of Christ. He is everything from a baby lying in a manger to a man crucified upon a Roman cross.

And he draws me.

Inside it is his mother, who is highly revered, though he is esteemed as well. Without him, after all, there is no "her."

I am drawn by water. Walls heavy laden and ceilings dripping with religious artwork, row upon row of pews, their patina rich and dark, pull me closer to the sound of water gushing into a small well below. Pulled into the cave like Chapel of the Spring, I come to rest above the water's source, and I peer over the railing to the place known as Mary's Spring where, they say, she came for water and received so much more.

I would dip my hand into it, if only I could reach it.

The water is clear and appears refreshing. Above it are more remembrances of Mary . . . of her life . . . of her gift.

Living Water.

Without him, Mary would have been just a girl. Just a virgin bride married to a Jewish carpenter. Just a mother like any other. Just like me. Without him, there was no "her."

Like her, without him, there is no *me*.

Above: *An eye-catching image adorns the marble floor in the parish church of the Basilica of the Annunciation.*

Left: Madonna and Child, *a gift from Japan, one of the representations of Mary and Jesus from different cultures around the world that adorn the walls of the parish church in the Basilica of the Annunciation. The Madonna's sleeve is made entirely of pearls.*

Left page: *Modern stained-glass windows cast a rainbow on the floor of the parish church.*

After the death of Moses the servant of the LORD, the LORD said to Joshua son of Nun, Moses' aide: "Moses my servant is dead. Now then, you and all these people, get ready to cross the Jordan River into the land I am about to give to them—to the Israelites. I will give you every place where you set your foot, as I promised Moses. Your territory will extend from the desert to Lebanon, and from the great river, the Euphrates—all the Hittite country—to the Great Sea on the west. No one will be able to stand up against you all the days of your life. As I was with Moses, so I will be with you; I will never leave you nor forsake you.

Joshua 1:1–5 NIV

About that time John the Baptist began preaching in the desert area of Judea. John said, "Change your hearts and lives because the kingdom of heaven is near." Many people came from Jerusalem and Judea and all the area around the Jordan River to hear John. They confessed their sins, and he baptized them in the Jordan River.

Matthew 3:1–2, 5–6

The Jordan River

The Jordan River rounds a bend and heads down the valley that bears its name, all the way to the Dead Sea.

from its beginning at Caesarea Philippi as
snowmelt from Mount Hermon to its end in
the Dead Sea 100 miles later. Only after it joins forces
with the Dan and the Hatzbani does it earn the name
"Jordan," surging wildly through steep basalt hills in the
Hula Valley at a pace dangerous enough to make hel-
meted rafters catch their breath. Slicing straight down
an artificial diversion channel created in the 1950s to
drain swamps, it then dips under the Daughters of Jacob
Bridge. Wending its way softly past Bethsaida, through
a jungle of reeds and brambles, it spills into the Sea of
Galilee, to feed Israel's most important water source.

The Jordan reappears near Yardenit, where pilgrims are baptized in calm waters, at the southern end of the Sea of Galilee. Here it begins its sixty-five-mile journey down the Jordan Valley, meandering its way through desolate marl plateaus as it charges past Adam—the place where the Jordan stopped flowing so the Children of Israel could cross (Joshua 3:16)—through the eastern Judean desert at Jericho, where it disappears into the Dead Sea.

Then Jesus came from Galilee to the Jordan to be baptized by John (Matthew 3:13 NIV). Here begins a great mystery for those who love the lore of this land. There seems to be no part of the Jordan River that has not at some time shouted, "Look at me! I am the place!" As the centuries flowed on, so did the traditions—north to south, east bank to west. The King James Version of John 1:28 mentions Bethabara, where the third-century church father Origen heard John did his baptizing. This may be Beth Barah of Judges 7:24, where Gideon's army chased the Midianites. Pursuing this stream of thought,

one late-nineteenth-century scholar[1] noted that around the time of the baptism, Jesus was with Galileans Peter, Andrew, and Philip, all from Bethsaida.

The baptismal site at Yardenit likes the northern possibility because the legend adds authenticity to the beauty and amenities here. However, we usually picture John preaching and baptizing not on such verdant banks, but in the desert (Matthew 3:1–5; Mark 1:4–5). So did early Christian pilgrims who sought a site "beyond the Jordan," on its eastern banks, opposite Jericho, where a church was first built in the early fifth century. That tradition never died out; in fact, it's enjoying a revival. But after the seventh-century Muslim conquest, when Christians limited their sacred circuit, many marked the baptism at a site later named Qasr al-Yahud ("the fortress of the Jews") across the river's thirty-foot span on the western side. This may be the one the pilgrim Egeria wrote about in the late fourth century, and Mark Twain visited there one chilly morning in 1867, giving his usual tongue-in-cheek take on the experience.[2]

In spite of the rushing waters at its source, it's never more than what you might call a creek. Yet the Jordan, from its source to its salty Dead Sea demise, deserves its title: the greatest river in Judeo-Christian history.

---

1 Benjamin B. Warfield, "The Scenes of the Baptist's Work." The Expositor 23 (1885) : 273–77. In *Selective Geographical Problems in the Life of Christ*, a doctoral dissertation by J. Carl Laney. Dallas Theological Seminary (1977) (posted as pdf file on www.bibleplaces.com).

2 Mark Twain. *The Innocents Abroad,* vol. 1. (New York and London n.d.), 339–342.

A eucalyptus bows its head gracefully on a tranquil stretch of the Jordan River at the baptismal site south of the Sea of Galilee.

 ark.

A river so murky the water reflects the overgrown foliage teetering over it like a black mirror. It looks more like a swamp to me than a river. For a time, I feel as though I've returned to the marshy banks of my Georgia youth rather than having come to the place where sin pours from the wet bodies dipped into the waters of forgiveness.

I wonder what drew me here. What, for that matter, has drawn all those who—only a few feet away—slip into the water for a chance to say they were baptized in the same river as Jesus.

A tear from heaven falls, landing on my forehead. I look up, then out to the gentle curve of the Jordan. The raindrops are few, but they send ripple after ripple to where birds have gathered in play. Wings spread out and

up, then *flap-flap-flap*. A few lift off. They fly low above the water, then dip lower still until they glide lazily over it. The rest remain in wait until their winged friends return and, once more, they travel along in a V-formation as they have always done and will always do.

I wonder again just what it was I came here to see. A river of shadows, so narrow I could skip a pebble over it if I barely tried? A group of pilgrims wanting to be more like Jesus? A flock of birds rejoicing in their own way over a precious few drops of rain?

It is no wonder I then think the water is so murky. Sin is the blackest form of dark. For thousands of years we've come to water—especially the Jordan—to slip in and dip under and be washed clean. *Wash me,* David wrote in Psalm 51:7, *and I will be whiter than snow.* We sometimes have difficulty understanding the *power*

Left page: A mother's joy shines forth after her baby is baptized in the Jordan River at the ancient site east of Jericho.

Below: Eastern Orthodox Christians gather at the banks of the Jordan near Jericho to celebrate the Epiphany at Jesus' baptism by John.

behind this concept, but we adhere to it nonetheless. We are, each of us and in our own time, drawn to the water of forgiveness.

I have much to be forgiven for, I think, as I sink to the damp boards of the walkway leading to the baptis-mal area. Sometimes I wonder if this river—from tip to tip—could begin to hold all the ugly that has darkened my heart and blackened my soul over the course of my lifetime. God alone knows what I have thought . . . what I have said . . . what I have done. God alone knows how desperately I need to be here.

I need to be at the banks of forgiveness every . . . single . . . day . . . of . . . my . . . life.

Another tear from heaven makes a rivulet down my cheek. I look up again, this time in understanding. *Tears of joy,* I think, *from God Himself.* Because I know why the people come. Why I have come.

And why I must return.

When Jesus heard that John had been put in prison, he went back to Galilee. He left Nazareth and went to live in Capernaum, a town near Lake Galilee, in the area near Zebulun and Naphtali. Jesus did this to bring about what the prophet Isaiah had said: "Land of Zebulun and land of Naphtali along the sea, beyond the Jordan River. This is Galilee where the non-Jewish people live. These people who live in darkness will see a great light. They live in a place covered with the shadows of death, but a light will shine on them." From that time Jesus began to preach, saying, "Change your hearts and lives, because the kingdom of heaven is near."

As Jesus was walking by Lake Galilee, he saw two brothers, Simon (called Peter) and his brother Andrew. They were throwing a net into the lake because they were fishermen. Jesus said, "Come follow me, and I will make you fish for people." So Simon and Andrew immediately left their nets and followed him. As Jesus continued walking by Lake Galilee, he saw two other brothers, James and John, the sons of Zebedee. They were in a boat with their father Zebedee, mending their nets. Jesus told them to come with him. Immediately they left the boat and their father, and they followed Jesus.

Jesus went everywhere in Galilee, teaching in the synagogues, preaching the Good News about the kingdom of heaven, and healing all the people's diseases and sicknesses. The news about Jesus spread all over Syria, and people brought all the sick to him. They were suffering from different kinds of diseases. Some were in great pain, some had demons, some were epileptics, and some were paralyzed. Jesus healed all of them. Many people from Galilee, the Ten Towns, Jerusalem, Judea, and the land across the Jordan River followed him.

Matthew 4:12–25

Mount Arbel

The land of Gennesaret, where Jesus preached and healed (Mark 6:53), stretches below Mount Arbel.

Sunset over Galilee, from Mount Arbel.

 t Mount Arbel, towering some one thousand feet above the Sea of Galilee, no vestiges of colorful mosaics have been discovered, no ruined churches or monasteries that elsewhere are sure indicators that long-ago Christians marked a site as sacred. On the contrary, only in recent years have Christians discovered the treasure that is Arbel, as they seek to look at the landscape the way Jesus did.

Matthew tells us that Jesus *left Nazareth and went to live in Capernaum, a town near Lake Galilee, in the area near Zebulon and Naphtali* (Matthew 4:13). This would have meant that from the tiny village of Nazareth, Jesus walked the main road leading from central Galilee's capital, Sepphoris, to Tiberias. That road passed Arbel, went through the Valley of Doves, met the Sea of Galilee, and continued north. It was so important that the opponents of Herod the Great took up posts in caves overlooking it, so they could disrupt traffic and hinder

Herod's rule. From these caves, according to the historian Josephus, they were routed out with a cruelty befitting the man who ordered the massacre of the innocents of Bethlehem.

Scripture mentions Arbel once, in the prophecy of Hosea 10:14, as *Beth Arbel*, the "House of Arbel." Many rabbis visited or studied at Arbel; the remains of a synagogue, dating from the second century AD, can still be seen, and the expanses that surround you as you climb toward the Arbel lookout once flourished with wheat and flax.

"Do you see the morning star?" a sage said to his friend as they walked through the Arbel Valley at dawn. "That is how Israel's salvation will begin, first slowly, and as redemption comes, so it becomes greater."[1] Medieval pilgrims on their way to the Sea of Galilee men-

---

1 Song of Songs Rabbah 6:10.

Mount Arbel sees dusk fall softly over the Sea of Galilee.

tion stopping at the tombs of the sons of Jacob and of his daughter, Dinah, over which they said myrtle plants flourished.

Now picture Jesus walking out to the edge of Mount Arbel where you, too, can stand, poised to begin the Galilee ministry. The fishing village of Magdala, home of Mary Magdalene, is just below. Beyond it to the north, the Valley of Gennesaret, "the ruler's garden," has rich soil and the anchorage where Jesus disembarked (Mark 6:53). Farther to the north are Korazin, Capernaum, and Bethsaida (home of Peter, Andrew, and Philip), which Jesus knew all too well (Matthew 11:21–24). The site of the Multiplication of Loaves and Fishes and the place of the miraculous catch of fish where Jesus appeared after the resurrection are both here. Along the "far shore" (John 6:1) on the east side of the lake, Jesus would also meet the needy crowds, and somewhere on slopes of the hills now called the Golan Heights is the land of the Gadarenes, where Jesus cast evil spirits into swine.

At Arbel, the heartland of the Gospels surrounds you, and an ancient pilgrimage phrase comes to life: "sacred geography."

y heart beats in wild anticipation.

I am about to climb the Arbel Cliff, as imposing a landmark as I've ever seen. It juts its chest out like a proud warrior and says, "Come up, and see what I see. Look over what I overlook. Peer into my craggy face and wonder at what protection I might provide. Come up and see."

I am climbing Arbel. Every so often I stop, take deep and uneven breaths, then begin again. Reaching the top of the cliff before sunset drives me onward and upward.

Once there, I take tentative steps over uneven terrain until I've come to the edge. Peering below to the Valley of Doves, my heart quickens in my throat, but not out of fear. I am more exhilarated at this moment than I have been in my life. There before me is what

may be the whole of Jesus' Galilean ministry. The path below is the one he took toward the Sea of Galilee, where fishermen—not knowing how their lives were about to change—performed their tasks. It stretches and curves from the area of his childhood toward the beginning of his ministry. There before me are the places he would preach, the town he would live in, and the sea where he would utter, "Follow Me," and people would drop what they were doing and pursue what they could not have imagined and had only dreamed of.

I, too, could not have begun to imagine. Not this vista, nor this lifetime of following him. Living with him. Loving him. Like the miles between where I now stand and the biblical sites below—sometimes rocky, other times a patchwork of fertile land—he and I have trekked

Left: *The setting sun glints through the branches of the single windblown oak atop Arbel.*

Right page: *An asphodel stands tall among the rocks on the path to Arbel.*

them together. Although I don't know what lies ahead around the bend of the sea, along the path, or up the hills and mountains, I trust him enough to drop it all and follow him.

My heart sings. The western sky has turned a blazing shade of gold as the sun sinks behind the Horns of Hattin, and I wonder at the magnificence of what my eyes behold. I can take photograph after photograph and never capture this moment, this setting of the sun. The ending of one day, the beginning of another.

Is this the mountain, I ask myself, *where Jesus came to his disciples and said, "Go and make followers of all people in the world and I will be with you"?* Until then, he had led and they had followed. Now, they would lead and others would follow.

Others like me.

My heart is heavy. It is time to go. To step down the jagged cliff and return to everyday life. But perhaps, like the eleven who remained, I can't do that now—having stood at the top of Arbel.

My heart goes on.

*N*ow when he saw the crowds, he went up on a mountainside and sat down. His disciples came to him, and he began to teach them saying: "Blessed . . ."

Matthew 5:1–3a NIV

Mount of Beatitudes

The Chapel of the Beatitudes crowns the traditional mountain where Jesus uttered the Sermon on the Mount.

Did You Know?

hat's in a name?

When Shakespeare's Romeo asked that question, he wanted to say that names did not matter. That's certainly not the case in the Holy Land, where you can be spiritually enriched by tracing the meanings of different names for the same place. The mountain with its breathtaking view of the Sea of Galilee is traditionally called the Mount of Beatitudes, a name bestowed by pilgrims over the generations who marked it as the site of the Sermon on the Mount as recorded in Matthew 5—7.

In the Latin translation of the Bible, the sermon begins with the word *beatitudini*, meaning "blessed are," repeated eight times. When Jesus spoke these words, he may have uttered the word *ashrei*, which means "happy." The word "happy" in this sense is also to be found in the original Hebrew of Psalm 1:1: *Happy are those who don't listen to the wicked, who don't go where sinners go, who don't do what evil people do.* It is found only rarely in English translations.

hen we adopt the moral and behavioral code of the Sermon on the Mount, an external event occurs—we are "blessed."

What can the difference between these two words, *happy* and *blessed*, tell us? When we adopt the moral and behavioral code of the Sermon on the Mount, an external event occurs—we are "blessed." But the original Hebrew tells us that our right actions precipitate an internal process—we are "happy." Many a sermon has em-phasized the inner process by interpreting these eight callings as the "be-attitudes"!

They love the Lord's teachings, and they think about those teachings day and night, Psalm 1 goes on to say. Those who heard Jesus' teachings in the Sermon on the Mount found in them the core of all Christian teachings and transmitted them through the generations until they were set down in writing. So significant were these words that they appear in two different versions in the Gospels: Matthew 5:7–9, their more extensive exposition, and a shorter version in Luke 6:17–49, often called the Sermon on the Plain.

Matthew often tells us that Jesus withdrew when he saw the crowds, and "his followers came to him." People often imagine Jesus speaking to crowds of people on this occasion, but were these followers the multitudes or the inner circle? The picture of the crowds especially suits Luke's description of the Sermon on the Plain. From the modern-day Chapel of the Beatitudes we can even see a likely location for this event—a point below where the mountain resolves itself into a plateau, now flourishing with bananas and loquat trees, before dipping down to the lakeshore. An often-told story among modern-day pilgrims seems to confirm the idea that the hillside was filled with people: at the right time of day and season, it says; an acoustical tunnel sends words spoken at the peak of the Mount of Beatitudes clearly all the way down to the lakeshore, four hundred feet below.

Perhaps Jesus spoke the extended sermon of Matthew to his inner circle, and then went down to the plain below, as Luke records it, to share with the spiritually thirsty who had gathered here from near and far.

Left: The altar in the sanctuary of the Chapel of the Beatitudes is surrounded by eight stained glass windows, each inscribed with one of the Beatitudes.

Above: Detail of a stained glass window in the Chapel of the Beatitudes: "Blessed are those who are persecuted because of righteousness, for theirs is the kingdom of heaven."

here is a gentle haze lying across the morning air. A chill permeates but does not make a body cold. Clouds, thick and cottony white, hang low in the sky, seeming to rest atop Arbel and play peekaboo with the hills surrounding Galilee. Flowers bloom in startling beauty of color and fullness, their petals dotted with dew. Standing on the Mount of Beatitudes, I am content—happy—within my surroundings. I find it difficult to be anything but.

Yet I know this is a fleeting moment. External contentment is based on life's current circumstances. It is the internal happiness Jesus spoke of when he said, *Blessed* . . .

The church here seems to throw back its shoulders against the hardship of life near the sea. Those who heard Jesus, it reminds me, were a folk who lived a peculiar life—free to come and go but not liberated. A people who needed to know that God had not forgotten them.

A people like me.

Happiness, I believe, comes from peace. Not peace in the land, for that is rare. Not the peace that ignited a movement forty years ago and inspired songs sung by long-haired men and women who painted flowers on their cheeks.

This is an internal, eternal peace. *Shalom.*

They say Jesus spoke here to those who were poor in spirit but teachable, those who lamented but sought God's righteousness, those who sought after peace but were instead persecuted, those who were merciful in spite of their personal unfulfilled needs, and those who kept the purity of heart I lost a long time ago—no matter what life had brought to them.

So pure, Jesus said, they would see the face of God.

Look again, my heart says. *They* saw *the face of God. It stood before them, preaching, teaching, and leading the way.*

I have stepped from the portico, with its glorious views of the sea and the plain, into the church. It is filled with seekers and followers who walk around the octagonal open hallway, peering into the church's central altar and gazing up at the eight stained glass windows with their Latin translation of each beatitude. Feet shuffle, prayers are whispered, and we stare in wonder at statues and artwork too aesthetic to touch or even linger before.

A hibiscus thrives in the tropical air in the garden of the Beatitudes near the Sea of Galilee.

A glimpse of the Galilee hills through a gate on the Mount of Beatitudes.

Blessed. It is as if the hallway whispers the word.

"So what do I do," I ask him, "to be so happy? With all life's cares and all life's woes? What do I do?"

Some say that it was here Jesus came to pray one night. And that, when morning came, he called all those who had been following him and, out of their number, called twelve in particular. He required they do more than follow. They were to carry the good news to others. Then, the Bible records, he spoke the words recorded in this church.

Perhaps, I now reason, the happiness comes not just in the knowing peace—*shalom*—but in sharing it with others.

Blessed.

When Jesus heard what had happened, he withdrew by boat privately to a solitary place. Hearing of this, the crowds followed him on foot from the towns. When Jesus landed and saw a large crowd, he had compassion on them and healed their sick. As evening approached, the disciples came to him and said, "This is a remote place, and it's already getting late. Send the crowds away, so they can go to the villages and buy themselves some food." Jesus replied, "They do not need to go away. You give them something to eat." "We have here only five loaves of bread and two fish," they answered. "Bring them here to me," he said. And he directed the people to sit down on the grass. Taking the five loaves and the two fish and looking up to heaven, he gave thanks and broke the loaves. Then he gave them to the disciples, and the disciples gave them to the people. They all ate and were satisfied, and the disciples picked up twelve basketfuls of broken pieces that were left over. The number of those who ate was about five thousand men, besides women and children.

Matthew 14:13–21 NIV

Church of the Multiplication of the Loaves and the Fishes

Looking up at the façade of the Church of the Multiplication of the Loaves and Fishes at Tabgha.

 hat do Sea-of-Galilee souvenir T-shirts, ashtrays, and an ancient holy site have in common? They are each adorned with a symbol that has survived for generations and still speaks to us today. But, of course, the holy site, the Church of the Multiplication, has the original: a small mosaic, in delicate shades of salmon and sand, depicting two fish flanking a basket of loaves with crosses in their centers.

This mosaic of loaves and fishes, the centerpiece of the church, is a sure sign that early Christians believed this was the place where Jesus fed the crowds of his followers with an amount of food equal to a little boy's lunch (John 6:9). The stories, categorized by scholars as the first and second multiplications, are rich and varied in detail—a crowd of five thousand (Matthew 14:13–21; Mark 6:31–44; Luke 9:10–17; John 6:1–12) and four thousand (Matthew 15:30–39; Mark 8:1–9), twelve leftover baskets (Matthew 14:20; Mark 6:43; Luke 9:17; John 6:13) and seven (Matthew 15:37; Mark 8:8), a lonely place (Mark 6:32) and a city (Luke 9:10). The details allow us to delve into many aspects of the two multiplication stories: their symbolism (twelve baskets represent the twelve tribes, or seven baskets represent each biblical nation), their geographical location (the west side of the lake near Capernaum or the north side of the lake near Bethsaida); and their ancient culture (five thousand men are fed in Luke 9:14, and women and children are included in Matthew 14:21; 15:38).

Left page: This fountain of seven fish in the courtyard of the church reminds us that the name Tabgha comes from the Greek word heptapegon, which means "seven springs."

The church honoring this miracle is in Tabgha (a form of the ancient Greek word *heptapegon* meaning "seven springs") and has been continually rebuilt until modern times. One of the seven springs, the spring of Job, still gushes just north of here at Ein Ayub. Here, we imagine, Christian travelers found respite, food, and water, and here they remembered the story.

Here, once again, we meet the fourth-century pilgrim Egeria. In her letter she wrote: "Overlooking the sea there is a grassy meadow full of many plants and palm trees, and near them the seven springs, that produce everlasting water: in this meadow the Lord fed the people with five loaves and two fishes. The stone on which the Lord laid the bread has become an altar, and nowadays visitors take away fragments of stone for their health and the wellbeing of all."[1]

A little mound of rock on which the faithful believe Jesus placed the bread still rises from behind the mosaic. It has survived all that chipping but has been darkened by millions of hands caressing it in an attempt to feel the spirit of that day. All accounts mention the blessing Jesus uttered. The blessing was doubtless a form of one eventually recorded in the Babylonian Talmud and still recited today: *Blessed are you O Lord our God, ruler of the universe, who brings forth bread from the earth.*[2]

That is the message the ancients have left you: Come here, remember, and give thanks.

---

2 Babylonian Talmud, Brachot 38a.

Trammel nets and cast nets are the nets most often mentioned in the Gospel fishing stories. Angling is only mentioned once, and unlike the Gospels' stories of miraculous catches of fish, the point of the story is not fishing as symbolism, but rather, Jesus' response to a challenge by the establishment, when the tax collectors ask Peter if Jesus pays Temple tax. Jesus answered, "go to the lake and fish. After you catch the first fish, open its mouth and you will find a coin. Take that coin and give it to the tax collectors for you and me'" (Matt. 17:27). Thus the name "St. Peter's fish" came into being. But although St. Peter's fish—tilapia, or fresh-water bass, is caught with nets, it is not attracted to bait. The only fish caught with hooks were barbel, a bottom-feeder and not a very attractive menu item for the many fish restaurants around the lake today. Thus, tilapia became the "St. Peter's fish" because it was good for tourism!*

* Mendel Nun. *The Sea of Galilee and its Fishermen in the New Testament*. (Kibbutz Ein Gev: 1989). 45-46.

---

1 Stanislau Loffreda, *The Sanctuaries of Tabgha* (Jerusalem: Franciscan Printing Press, 1978), 16.

am hungry.

The morning's meal has long been forgotten as my stomach begins to rumble. But the midday meal must wait because we have come to the place where, they say, Jesus fed more than most can comprehend for a picnic. Five thousand men, not counting women and children, fed. And twelve basketfuls of broken pieces left over. Jesus met the physical need of a crowd when, in fact, his heart was breaking and he needed time to be alone with his thoughts.

I am in the breezeway of the chapel at Tabgha known as the Church of the Multiplication of the Loaves and the Fishes. Each step I take toward the chapel echoes in the wide expanse of white stone archways; those to the left lead to the center courtyard, where the mouths of seven ornamental fish trickle water as a reminder of the seven springs nearby. Above my head, flighty birds swoop and play in the wooden rafters from which their thinning nests spill over. At the end of the long walkway, a single word hangs from the final arch: *Silence.*

Here, I think, *two thousand years ago, it would have been anything but silent.*

Inside the chapel, I am struck by many things: The flourish of symbols beneath my feet. The unique mosaic floor unlike any I've seen before. The holy water near the doors. The flickering of novenas. A lack of furnishings flanked by holy pictures. The dizzying immensity of the space. The blackened stone beneath the simple altar. The intricate mosaic of a bread-filled basket rising between two fish.

We only have five loaves, the disciples told Jesus. *We only have two fish.*

Left: *The famed Byzantine mosaic of the Loaves and Fishes.*

Right page: *The breezeway leading to the sanctuary of Tabgha's Church of the Multiplication of the Loaves and the Fishes on the Sea of Galilee.*

Isn't this the way of it? We think of what we "only have" rather than what it might become in Jesus' hands. Not enough, we think, and so we hold back. We hold to ourselves, even. With this, we think, we must feed ourselves only because we are hungry.

I sink to the cold stone of the floor; my chin dips toward my chest.

I am guilty, I realize, of holding on to what I have. Not trusting my Lord with what I've got. I stretch my hand toward the lump of rugged stone beneath the altar. If only I *could* place what little I have to offer upon it, Jesus *would* feed others.

Jesus would feed me.

I close my eyes and see him miraculously multiplying the few until it became the many. The little until it became the much. And whom should he feed first?

The boy, or so I imagine. And what does the boy do, then, with the broken pieces left over? Take them home to feed his poor family. And what should the disciples do when the multitudes come hungry again? They doubt.

But I see Jesus smile at them as he gently asks, "How many loaves do you have?"

Maybe they understood? Maybe I understand that whatever the number, in his hands it is always enough.

When the people found Jesus on the other side of the lake, they asked him, "Teacher, when did you come here?"

Jesus answered, "I tell you the truth, you aren't looking for me because you saw me do miracles. You are looking for me because you ate the bread and were satisfied . . ."

The people asked Jesus, "What are the things God wants us to do?"

Jesus answered, " . . . believe . . . ."

So the people asked, "What miracle will you do? If we see a miracle, we will believe you. What will you do? . . . Our ancestors ate the manna in the desert . . ."

Jesus said, "I tell you the truth, it was not Moses who gave you bread from heaven, but it is my Father who is giving you the true bread from heaven. . . ."

"Sir, give us this bread always."

Then Jesus said, "I am the bread . . . ."

Excerpted from John 6:25–35

Capernaum

The ancient synagogue at Capernaum, built over the synagogue where Jesus preached and healed.

apernaum means "village of Nahum," but we cannot be certain who this particular Nahum was or when the town was founded. Some have seen symbolism in this name, which in Hebrew means comfort, recalling the many miracles of healing Jesus performed in this vicinity.

Thanks to the archaeologists who excavated the ruins of Capernaum during the twentieth century, we can picture it as a bustling town where fishermen hauling in their catch rubbed elbows with Galilean farmers marketing their harvest or waiting for their olives to be pressed into oil. Women are hard at work in the courtyards, grinding grain , baking their daily bread, or weaving the clothing for their families. A royal official healed by Jesus (John 4:46) probably lived in the wealthier part of town, where a fine bathhouse was uncovered. The centurion, placed by Luke and Matthew in Capernaum, indicates the presence of at least one hundred Roman soldiers. Matthew may have even known him personally, as the centurion's men would have guarded the tax money he collected.

Two jewels in Capernaum's crown have come to light: the synagogue and Peter's house. The synagogue, the last phases of whose construction date from the fourth or fifth century AD,[1] is known as "the white synagogue" because of its massive limestone columns that gleam in the Galilean sun. It is truly a place where, in the words of the old hymn, you can walk where Jesus walked; many believe it stands on the exact spot where Jesus taught and performed miracles.

From the synagogue, Jesus and the disciples set out for Peter's mother-in-law's house, where she lay ill with a fever (Mark 1:29–30). Between the synagogue and Peter's house, archaeologists have found the remains of many homes that give us a good idea of the way Peter's would have looked. It probably consisted of one room, perhaps divided by rough-hewn pillars that separated the living area from a kind of a pantry-storage room. Such homes were clustered around central courtyards, where the baking ovens were located. No roofs are left, but the stone steps leading to them are still in place. We know from archaeological discoveries and from homes in traditional villages throughout the Bible lands today that the roof was flat, made of packed earth and straw, and supported by wooden or stone rafters. The men who brought their paralyzed neighbor to be healed by Jesus would have had to dig through this material (Mark 2:4) to reach their rabbi.

Early Christians made it easy for us to identify Peter's house: around one simple dwelling they built a massive octagonal church in the fourth century, refurbishing and enlarging it about a century later. The most exciting discovery in this dwelling was a group of 131 inscriptions scratched into its plaster walls by pilgrims in Greek, Aramaic, Latin, and the ancient Semitic language Syriac. Many of the inscriptions bless the name of Jesus and ask God's mercy. The realization that this may have been the site of one of the first house-churches in the Christian world is thrilling for today's Christian visitors.

Right page: *A reconstructed doorway of the Capernaum synagogue, frames the modern Memorial of St. Peter, built over the traditional house of Peter's mother-in-law.*

1 Vassilios Tzaferis. Capernaum. *The New Encyclopedia of the Archaeology of the Holy Land.* (1993), 291–296.

131

t is a city of miracles and teaching. A place where men were called and they followed. It is the town by the sea which Jesus called "home." It is where five of the twelve disciples—Peter, Andrew, James, John, and Matthew—lived, were called, and chose to follow. This is where the sick and desperate sought him out. This is where those who were hungry in spirit came to feast on words spoken by the One who claimed to be the "Bread of Life" and where Jesus spoke a word that has reverberated through the centuries: *Believe.*

It is also a most remarkable place, a place bursting with life among the stone ruins and the blue shimmer of the ancient sea. Brilliantly colored flowers spill over crumbling walls and decorate a preserved olive press along the walkway leading to the synagogue, which boasts a section of first-century flooring flanked by elaborately carved limestone columns. Here, it is believed, Jesus taught and amazed the people who came to hear this ordinary carpenter from Galilee; a man who spoke as one with authority. Here, it is supposed, a demon-possessed man cried out, "Jesus of Nazareth! What do you want with us?"

Standing here today in the shade of old buildings and trees thick with foliage, I hear my heart as it cries out nearly those very same words. *Jesus of Nazareth, what do you want with me?* it inquires as though from the very core of my being.

I want you to believe, his Spirit whispers back.

Here in Capernaum, believing is easy. Even the entrance gate boasts a sign that reads: *The Town of Jesus.* The evidence of God is everywhere from the racks of tourists' books near the entryway, to the gentle (though sometimes fierce) lapping of waves from the Sea of Galilee, and back to the Franciscan octagonal Byzantine church that rests above the home of Peter. Dipping my head to look beneath it, I see Jesus with my mind's eye. He is touching Peter's mother-in-law and commanding, "Be well." And she was, in that moment, healed.

But did she, I wonder, believe *before* she was healed?

Here, in Capernaum, I hear another question, an even more difficult one. Not from my heart to me, but from my heart to God. *What do you want with me? Beyond belief . . . beyond believing . . .*

Between the synagogue and the Byzantine church is the olive press boasting black asphalt millstones undestroyed by time. I step over to the rose-colored wrought iron gate around them and, gripping the iron, lean in to study them. As they gleam in the sun's light, they bring to mind words Jesus spoke here: *If one of these little children believes in me, and someone causes that child to sin, it would be better for that person to have a large [mill]stone tied around the neck and be drowned in the sea.*

Standing here now, I determine that—like an unquestioning child—I *want* to believe. Beyond believing, I want to live as though I do.

Left: *A reconstructed colonnade stands tall among the ruins of the synagogue of Capernaum.*

Left page: *Beneath the Memorial of St. Peter are the remains of what is traditionally said to be the house of Peter's mother-in-law in Capernaum.*

$\mathcal{I}$mmediately [after the feeding of the five thousand] Jesus told his followers to get into the boat and go ahead of him to Bethsaida across the lake. He stayed there to send the people home. After sending them away, he went into the hills to pray. That night, the boat was in the middle of the lake, and Jesus was alone on the land. He saw his followers struggling hard to row the boat, because the wind was blowing against them. Between three and six o'clock in the morning, Jesus came to them, walking on the water, and he wanted to walk past the boat. But when they saw him walking on the water, they thought he was a ghost and cried out. They all saw him and were afraid. But quickly Jesus spoke to them and said, "Have courage! It is I."

Mark 6:45–50

There were some Greek people, too, who came to Jerusalem to worship at the Passover Feast. They went to Philip, who was from Bethsaida in Galilee, and said, "Sir, we would like to see Jesus."

John 12:20–21

Bethsaida

A view of a first-century street at Bethsaida.

ethsaida was a place of miracles. A blind man was healed here (Mark 8:22) and, according to Luke 9:10–17, this was the location of the miraculous feeding of the five thousand.

Some of Jesus' closest companions hailed from here: Peter, Andrew, and Philip (John 1:44). Jesus knew Bethsaida well enough to warn its inhabitants of a woeful future because of their disbelief (Matthew 11:21). What Christian would not want to walk the paths of this village?

Pilgrims did stream to Bethsaida in the early days of Christianity. But as the perils of the journey became too great to bear, their visits ceased. And Bethsaida, forgotten, disappeared from the face of the earth.

Or so it seemed. Then, in the late 1980s, Professor Rami Arav of the University of Omaha in Nebraska, zeroed in on a huge, twenty-one-acre mound of ruins a mile or so north of the Sea of Galilee. Bethsaida of the Gospels was back on the map.

A visit to Bethsaida, especially in the summer, when the archaeologists are at work, is everything that reflecting on the Bible is all about. The excitement of rediscovering the distant past is matched only by the realization that until just a few decades ago, no one knew that long-lost Bethsaida, with its scriptural treasures, would reveal itself. Now you can have the rare privilege of walking along a street from Jesus' time, its rough cobblestones still entrenched where they were first laid.

The excavations of Bethsaida also unearthed a fisherman's house, identified by a fishing net's weight stone, a stone anchor, a fishhook, and a needle for sewing nets. It reminds us of the fishermen-disciples who called this town home. In the vintner's house next door, the sickles for harvesting grapes and hooks for carrying them were still stored in the basement.

Among the newest information to emerge from the Bethsaida excavations is the date of its founding as a Jewish community—about the time of Herod the Great, between 25 and 10 BC, when Jews from Judea came to what by then was an abandoned village. Nazareth (as well as Nain and Cana) were also settled by Judeans at this time. Thus Jesus' family would have come in from Judea, David's home territory, as virtually all the Jews in Galilee did in this period.

Bethsaida has also been identified as an important Old Testament site, the likely capital of the kingdom of Geshur (Joshua 13:11; 1 Chronicles 2:23). David

s you stand on the summit of Tel Bethsaida, at your feet are the jumbled ruins of its massive gateway, likely laid waste by the Assyrians, and the Sea of Galilee glistens in the distance. The verse of an old poem, which many a schoolchild learned by heart in another time, comes to mind: "The Destruction of Sennacherib" by Lord Byron:

The Assyrian came down like a wolf on the fold,
And his cohorts were gleaming in purple and gold;
And the sheen of their spears was like stars on the sea,
When the blue wave rolls nightly on deep Galilee.*

*With thanks to Don and Loretta Vargo

Wherever he went, to village or town or farm, they laid the sick in the streets and begged him to let them simply touch the edge of his cloak; and all who touched him were healed.

Mark 6:56

was a valiant young warrior when he married Maacah, the daughter of this city's king (2 Samuel 3:3). Thus, Absalom, their son, fled here, to the land of his paternal grandfather, from David's wrath.

Monumental gates of those days were also found here. In 732 BC they were engulfed by a huge fire so hot it changed the mud brick into glass. Just like the power of Bethsaida itself, the fire burned its way through the veil of history, changing and enriching our understanding of this Holy Land.

A pillar is erected on a street of Bethsaida, inscribed with words from Mark's gospel. Just over the stone wall, the Sea of Galilee shimmers near this fishing village.

137

 t is no more than a narrow bend in the road. Before it, gravel laid by modern men. Behind it, the same. But there, in the bend, is an inset of large rocks—stones, if you will—that have been traversed for more than two thousand years.

It takes a moment for the significance to sink in.

I turn back, for I nearly missed it, and—kneeling there—whisper a simple prayer. *Remind me, Lord. My footsteps follow yours. Yours do not follow mine. Help me to know you better, to recognize what you attempt to show me.*

I am on the road to Bethsaida, following in the footsteps of Jesus and those who wished to see him. Though it boasts the largest city gate from the Iron Age and held some of Israel's largest homes in antiquity, its ruins have been uncovered for fewer than thirty years. Until recent days, man seemed to have forgotten the home of the fishermen—Peter, Andrew, and Philip—the place where Jesus healed the blind man. This was the place where he sent his disciples after feeding the five thousand, only to lead them directly into a storm.

The city about which he cried out, *"Woe to you, Bethsaida!"*

Standing just inside the gate, looking out over the rugged, time-baked ruins, I wonder why.

Because they saw the miracles, but did not repent, the Word tells me.

How can so much that is right, and so much that is wrong, come out of the same place? Not just this city, or Korazin or Capernaum. I am thinking only of myself.

I am sitting outside the city gates. From overhead a large tree casts its shade upon me. I feel peace, in spite of the turmoil that wiped the thriving Bethsaida from Israel's landscape, because I know my soul has repented and Jesus heard that cry.

History's voice echoes from the sea, across the valley, and up to the hillside where I sit: "We would like to see Jesus."

I would like to see Jesus.

I have stepped in my Reeboks where sandaled feet once shuffled by. I have looked out over the sea where bare feet walked on waves as though they were stepping-stones. I have seen the ruins of a township that failed to heed the call to repentance. But have I *seen* Jesus?

I want to know Christ, Paul wrote to the Philippians (3:10).

I begin my walk back down the hill. Then, it comes to me. A voice so loud, at first I think it is from someone standing behind me. "Yeshua!" it cries out. I whip my head around, but there is no one there. Just the shimmering of the trees, the glint on the stone in the noonday sun, and the shadows on the ground chasing fragments of light left behind.

I turn again. But I am alone. It is just me. *And him.*

I run to my friend and say, "His name. His name . . . his name is *Yeshua!"*

And I smile. Because I now know what the stones in the road and the rocks of the ruins tried to say to me. *To know him, to understand his ways, is first to know his name.*

Jesus, Peter, Andrew and Philip could have walked on the very stones of this Bethsaida lane.

Soon afterwards Jesus went to a town called Nain, and his followers and a large crowd traveled with him. When he came near the town gate, he saw a funeral. A mother, who was a widow, had lost her only son. A large crowd from the town was with the mother while her son was being carried out. When the Lord saw her, he felt very sorry for her and said, "Don't cry." He went up and touched the coffin, and the people who were carrying it stopped. Jesus said, "Young man, I tell you, get up!" And the son sat up and began to talk. Then Jesus gave him back to his mother.

Luke 7:11–15

The thief does not come except to steal, and to kill, and to destroy. I have come that they may have life, and that they may have it more abundantly.

John 10:10 NKJV

Nain

The façade of the late 19th century church at Nain. Near the corner of the church stands an ancient stone coffin to remind us of the resurrection of the widow's son (although the coffin in the story of Nain, carried by neighbors, would have been a wooden one).

esus would have called Nain, where he raised a widow's son from the dead, by the Hebrew form of its name, *Na'im,* which means "pleasant." That name still describes this village, nestled at the foot of the north slope of Mount Moreh amid the green fields of the Jezreel Valley stretching past Mount Tabor to the Nazareth Mountains. Today it is a Muslim village of approximately 1,800 inhabitants, their spacious homes lining its streets, one of which leads to the Catholic church that marks the site of the miracle. The key to the church, which shares a parking lot with Nain's mosque, is given to visitors by the Muslim caretaker who lives next door.

srael Antiquities Authority (IAA) excavations in Nain have unearthed a Roman-era building faced with dressed stone and containing a number of rooms. A thick layer of charcoal was found on the walls and floors of the building, apparently remnants of a huge fire that consumed its wooden portions. The fire caused the building to collapse, burying the inhabitants beneath. Next to their skeletal remains, gold and silver jewelry were found, as well as the daily vessels they used. Archaeologists cannot say for sure whether the Romans set fire to the structure during the Great Revolt in AD 67 in their campaign against the Jews of Nain, or whether the fire was precipitated by an earthquake. Either way, "the destruction was so sudden and total that the inhabitants did not stand a chance," dig director Fadi Abu-Zeidan told the press.

In Jesus' day Nain was probably one of 240 "cities and villages" that historian Flavius Josephus writes were in Galilee.[1] It was probably not one of the region's poorer communities, since its residents built expensive walls around it (Luke 7:12). Such cities would have been about ten acres in size, with a population perhaps reaching one thousand people.

For a widow living in Nain two thousand years ago, town life could be harder than village life. In the farming village, extended families were self-sufficient. Women held a powerful position on such a homestead, in charge of at least two important areas of home production—bread and cloth. A woman also might have tended her own vegetable patch near her home, and she could sell or barter the fruit of her labors in that garden to supplement the allowance she received from her husband.

In town, however, things could be very different. A town-dwelling woman usually had to buy her bread from the baker, not make it herself, and the same was true for other commodities. Perhaps her husband provided some service to the town or its rural hinterland; he may have been the town blacksmith or carpenter or a teacher of children in the synagogue.

And what about an unmarried woman like the widow of Nain? A younger widow could go back to her father's house, where a room would be added onto the house for her. An older widow would hopefully have at least one son to support her, one reason why Psalm 113:9 literally reads *a mother of sons is happy.* But a sonless

1 Josephus Flavius *Life* 45.235.

widow could face disaster. That is why biblical law mandates care for widows (Deuteronomy 10:18; 24:17; Isaiah 1:17), a rule the early Christian communities took very seriously (1 Timothy 5:3).

The widow of Nain perhaps wept not only for the loss of the son she had raised and loved, but also out of fear for her uncertain future. Thus we can understand

The ornate altar in the church of Nain stands in stark contrast to the threadbare sanctuary.

Luke's words, *Then Jesus gave him back to his mother* (7:15) as not only restoring the comfort and affection of her son, and not only her standing in the community, but very likely life itself.

We take slow steps into the courtyard, where a young man—the caretaker's son?—tinkers with an old motor. As my friend asks about going inside the chapel, I take a few more tentative steps to the left side of the church. There I look past a chicken coop to the green of the valley and the unmistakable shape of Mount Tabor. A rooster crows at midday, welcoming *anyone* who might wander by, enter in, and witness a memorial to true compassion.

We enter, and my disbelief gives way to something more. Something I cannot fathom. Two rows of ten plastic chairs face each other, making a wide path to the altar. We move toward it as though we have entered another time or place. Black and white marble floors are scarred and faded. We crane our necks and look overhead to the high windows shrouded by dirt and cobwebs. In spite of this, the small altar is spectacular and intricate in design. The massive paintings behind it and before it are rich in detail. They depict the raising of the widow's son.

This act was nearly forgotten. Abandoned. Cast aside like the empty ossuary outside the front door. It is as if no one comes. Or ever came.

And yet, I know that they do, they did . . . he did. I know that there was a woman who buried her husband and then faced the grief of burying her son. For the people in his funeral procession, it was but another of life's passages, mournfully marked. But for his mother, it was her very existence. Who would care for her? Where would she live? *How* would she live? At her most desperate, would she become a prostitute, sold to a man for his pleasure?

And I know that Jesus, moved by what he saw, went out of his way to restore life to the woman's son. And to the mother in the process.

 stare in disbelief at the tiny church near the top of a winding incline. Outside, it is nondescript, except to say that with its two arched windows and narrow double doors, it reminds me of a face, opening its mouth and eyes in horror. *Perhaps this is like the emotion felt by the woman who lived in this village two thousand years ago*, I think. Life had played a monstrous trick on her, ripping her very existence in two and shattering her world as she knew it. Her only son was dead.

Left: A painting in the church at Nain depicts Jesus raising the widow's son from the dead at the town gate.

Left page: Seen through the church door at Nain, a rooster pecks for kernels in the courtyard, over the ground on which Jesus once walked.

I understand the woman. I, too, have felt life's grief. I have known the heartache of feeling alone and vulnerable. Not to a man, no. But to sin, yes. Facing tomorrow and tomorrow's tomorrows with stumbling steps.

And I know what it means to have Jesus go out of his way to give life back to me. A life of abundance and joy, of meaning and fulfillment. Not shrouded like the windows or scarred like these floors. Not forgotten like the ossuary. Rather, a life—because of the touch of Jesus—like the altar: intricate in design. Like the paintings: rich in detail.

𝒟eborah sent a message to Barak son of Abinoam . . . Deborah said to Barak, "The LORD, the God of Israel, commands you: 'Go and gather ten thousand men of Naphtali and Zebulun and lead them to Mount Tabor. I will make Sisera, the commander of Jabin's army, and his chariots, and his army meet you at the Kishon River. I will hand Sisera over to you.'" Then Barak said to Deborah, "I will go if you will go with me, but if you won't go with me, I won't go." "Of course I will go with you," Deborah answered, "but you will not get credit for the victory. The LORD will let a woman defeat Sisera." So Deborah went with Barak to Kedesh. At Kedesh, Barak called the people of Zebulun and Naphtali together. From them, he gathered ten thousand men to follow him, and Deborah went with him also . . . When Sisera was told that Barak son of Abinoam had gone to Mount Tabor, Sisera gathered his nine hundred iron chariots and all the men with him, from Harosheth Haggoyim to the Kishon River. Then Deborah said to Barak, "Get up! Today is the day the LORD will hand over Sisera. The LORD has already cleared the way for you." So Barak led ten thousand men down Mount Tabor.

Excerpted from Judges 4:6–14

Six days later, Jesus took Peter, James, and John, the brother of James, up on a high mountain by themselves. While they watched, Jesus' appearance was changed; his face became bright like the sun, and his clothes became white as light. Then Moses and Elijah appeared to them, talking with Jesus. Peter said to Jesus, "Lord, it is good that we are here. If you want, I will put up three tents here—one for you, one for Moses, and one for Elijah." While Peter was talking, a bright cloud covered them. A voice came from the cloud and said, "This is my Son, whom I love, and I am very pleased with him. Listen to him!" When his followers heard the voice, they were so frightened they fell to the ground. But Jesus went to them and touched them and said, "Stand up. Don't be afraid."

Matthew 17:1–7

Mount Tabor and Mount Hermon sing for joy at your name.

Psalm 89:12b

Mount Tabor

*Mount Tabor, with the Church of the Transfiguration on the summit,
stands watch over the homes of the village of Nain in the foreground.*

Did You Know?

hat a need we have to mark our place in the world. No sooner had the brilliant moment of the Transfiguration passed than Peter waxed architectural: *Lord, it is good that we are here. If you want, I will put up three tents here—one for you, one for Moses, and one for Elijah* (Matthew 17:4).

Perhaps Peter did put up his tents, or at least mounds of stones to mark the event, as is the custom in this rock-filled land. In any case, the mountain of the Transfiguration is recorded only as a "high mountain." We are drawn to Mount Tabor as the spot by the signposts of the Hebrew Scriptures, and in the footsteps of early Christian travelers, who eventually did build a great tabernacle of prayer here: the Church of the Transfiguration.

Architectural markers are nothing more than attempts to imitate nature's more wondrous points of reference, of which Mount Tabor is certainly one. It was a landmark for the borders of three tribes: Zebulun in the west, Issachar in the south, and Naphtali in the north. These tribal inheritances live up to Jacob's blessings (Genesis 49:13–14, 21), exuding the abundance and beauty from which Mount Tabor rises, perfectly round, some 1,400 feet above the fertile Jezreel Valley.

War first barges into this pastoral landscape when Deborah has her general, Barak, call the Israelite tribes together to battle the Canaanites, sweeping down on them as they amassed in the flatlands (Judges 4:14–16). And like Carmel, and other tree-covered slopes in the Holy Land, Tabor's beauty was a snare entrapping the

Right: The entrance to the Church of the Transfiguration. The towers on either side of the doorway are said to symbolize Moses and Elijah.

Left page: The snow-covered peak of "grandfather Hermon" as it is nicknamed, crowns Israel at its northernmost point.

Israelites in idol worship (Hosea 5:1). Jeremiah embroils this beautiful site in warlike imagery depicting the king of Babylon coming *like Tabor among the mountains* (Jeremiah 46:18). Early in their conquest the Romans defeated the Jews in Tabor's shadow, killing ten thousand.[1]

War is not the only tale that pre-Transfiguration Tabor tells. It rises from the plain in splendid isolation, but its mountain companions share its glory. One legend relates: "When the Holy One, blessed be he, sought to give the Torah to Israel at Sinai, the mountains came running and quarreling with one another . . . Tabor . . . and Carmel . . . 'As I live, says the King whose name is the Lord of hosts, surely like Tabor among the mountains and like Carmel by the sea shall he come.'"[2]

Psalm 89:12 unites Tabor with another mountain peak in praise of God: *You created the north and the south: Mount Tabor and Mount Hermon sing for joy at your name.* If season and weather are in your favor the day you climb Tabor, you see the very view that inspired the psalmist: the snowcapped peak of Mount Hermon floating above the clouds eighty miles to the north.

And then in a pure place beyond war and beyond boundaries, in a shimmering moment of transfiguration, you too can say with simple wonder: *His glory fills the whole earth* (Isaiah 6:3).

---

1 Josephus Flavius. *The Wars of the Jews* 1.8.177.

2 *Genesis Rabbah* 99.1 (ref. Jeremiah 46.18).

he road to the top of the mountain is steep. Winding. It's as if we are on God's roller coaster, going up and around. In comparison to Mount Hermon, Mount Tabor seems only a lump on the land. But with each turn of the wheel, it becomes apparent why Deborah chose this as her lookout and Jesus as his place of glorious display.

If this is, in fact, where the Transfiguration occurred.

Not that it matters, really. Some say Tabor, some say Hermon, and some say another mountain. The "where" doesn't mean anything when laid against the "what" or the "who."

Inside the church is art in all its wonder. Mosaics and light. Marble and stone. Brightest gold. Purest white. Three angels forever stand guard over a babe, asleep in a manger. Three others offer adoration to a sleeping lamb. Three stand, lifting holy hands, one containing the holy Eucharist. Three more stand over and near an empty tomb.

The crypt is illuminated by the sun's light pouring through stained glass, and proud peacocks peer over their shoulders. The colors around them and through them are as brilliant as any displayed by nature.

I am in awe. I am as transfixed as he was transfigured. The air inside the church is heavy with an anticipation I'd not expected. As though at any minute, some illumination might burst through and change all who enter. All who, regrettably, must return to the base of the mountain. Just as Peter did. Just as James and John.

That which was from the beginning, which we have heard, John wrote in his first letter (1:1 NIV).

We ourselves heard this voice that came from heaven when we were with him on the sacred mountain, Peter wrote in his second letter (1:18 NIV).

But, I am alone here, unlike the disciples. Most certainly unlike Jesus, standing between Moses and Elijah. The Law and the Prophets.

Do not think that I have come to abolish the Law or the Prophets; I have not come to abolish them but to fulfill them (Matthew 5:17 NIV).

I walk toward the altar, taking the few steps down, then looking up. Above my head *Et transfiguratus est ante eos* is engraved in Latin. I don't know what it says. But I do know what it means.

I hear a whisper of a sound. I turn. Someone has left one of the doors ajar at the front of the church, and a light—brilliant and strangely fragmented—has exploded through the opening. I gasp, then hold my breath at the loveliness of it. I listen for a voice—a still, small voice—to say, *Tell no one of this,* but it doesn't come. I wait, then, for the light to pass, even as the sun slips behind a cloud. I bound up the stairs, up the center aisle, and out to the area leading to the gardens.

I rejoin my friend, and we talk about what we have seen. What we have heard. What our hands have touched. Then I look north. I point, and I smile.

Hermon. Shouting for joy with Tabor! Hermon!

Left: *Jesus transfigured is depicted in this magnificent mosaic adorning the apse of the church on Mount Tabor. He is flanked by Moses and Elijah on clouds, with Peter, James, and John below them.*

Left page: *"Jerusalem Crosses," the symbol of the Franciscan order, surround a cross adorning the ceiling of the Church of Transfiguration.*

As Jesus was walking beside the Sea of Galilee, he saw two brothers, Simon called Peter and his brother Andrew. They were casting a net into the lake, for they were fishermen. "Come, follow me," Jesus said, "and I will make you fishers of men." At once they left their nets and followed him. Going on from there, he saw two other brothers, James son of Zebedee and his brother John. They were in a boat with their father Zebedee, preparing their nets. Jesus called them, and immediately they left the boat and their father and followed him.

Matthew 4:18–22 NIV

The Galilee Boat

The Galilee Boat on display on a "sea" of glass, with an ancient mosaic of a boat depicted on the wall behind it.

hat craft sails every day on the high seas of gospel history, but has not been boarded for two thousand years? It is the Galilee Boat, a vessel from the time of Jesus that is the centerpiece of a magnificent museum display on the western shore of the Sea of Galilee.

So many images that Christians are raised on come to mind when looking at this boat: Peter stepping out of a boat to walk on the water (Matthew 14:30) or impulsively jumping out, the faster to reach shore and the resurrected Jesus he saw there (John 21:7); Jesus calming the storm (Luke 8:22–25) or preaching from a boat to the people gathered on shore (Luke 5:3); the disciples throwing their net over the other side of the boat and pulling up a miraculous catch of fish (John 21:6).

When fishermen brothers Moshe and Yuvi Lufan discovered this wooden boat in 1986, mired in the mud on the shores of a drought-depleted Sea of Galilee, they could hardly have imagined how magnificent it would look now, proudly restored and on display. They could not have known at the start how meaningful it would be to the nearly one million visitors who have seen it over the years. For this wooden boat, one of the few authentic objects conclusively dated to the first century, has the power to evoke the life and times of Jesus as never before.

The boat is about 24 feet long, 7 feet wide, and a little less than 4 feet deep. It was built using the "shell first" technique, with mortise and tenon joinery. Cedar and oak make up most of the boat's planks and frame, but there are ten other kinds of wood. A tribute to the imagination of the display's designers is the planting of one of each of these species on the path leading to

Right page: A bowl discovered in the boat, whose form helps date it to the first century CE.

the museum. The ancient craftsmen removed much of the wood from older boats, which attests to repeated repair, perhaps over many decades. It was large enough to carry 15 people, including a crew of five. Though apparently used for fishing, it may also have transported passengers and goods.

The construction technique, along with two pottery vessels found nearby, has led archaeologists to conclude that the boat dates from the Roman period. Experts report that Carbon-14 tests confirm that the boat had been constructed and used between 100 BC and AD 70.[1] The boat was in an amazing state of preservation, thanks to its having been encased for two thousand years in mud, where wood-devouring bacteria cannot breathe. It was completely waterlogged when found, and in order to keep it from crumbling into dust, it was immediately immersed in a giant tub. Over a period of years the water-soluble wax that now binds it together was added to its bath. Such preservation had never before been attempted, and its success is a tribute to scientific ingenuity as well as love for the sacred history of the boat and the Holy Land.

1 Israel Carmi, "Radiocarbon Dating of the Boat" in *The Excavations of an Ancient Boat in the Sea of Galilee (Lake Kinneret) 'Atiqot* 19 (Israel Antiquities Authority: 1990). 127.

An empty boat.

A fragment of a boat, really. Displayed against a rotating picture so as to compare what it is today to what it was two thousand years ago. Around it is a mesmerizing, modern museum of the highest caliber. Rounded glass tinted in sea green—layered row upon row—gives the illusion of the boat floating on the Sea of Galilee, which is only a few feet away, shimmering in the afternoon sun. Nearby, sealed glass cases keep safe the precious cargo found within and without the boat.

Who, I wonder, *sat in this boat? Worked in this boat? Slept in this boat? Leapt out of this boat for any number of reasons?*

And what led to its abandonment? For the boat was—for whatever reason—abandoned. Left to be found by two brothers who woke one morning thinking it was a day like any other day, only to be remarkably surprised by their discovery along the shores of Galilee.

Two brothers. Like Peter and Andrew or James and John. Fishermen, all six men. Bound by occupation and

Left page: *The double rainbow that appeared over the Sea of Galilee when the boat was discovered.*

history and tales of the water in the sea. What Moshe and Yuval Lufan found may be what Peter and Andrew or James and John left behind.

I step outside to the place where the sea gently laps against the shoreline. It is, I think, almost lonely here. The sun warms my skin as it slips toward the heights across the lake. I turn my face and, closing my eyes, feel a breeze as it kisses my cheeks.

Follow me.

I hear the words. I know their history. Their simplicity. Their complexity.

"Follow me," I know, means more than falling behind someone who is walking before you. "Follow me" means leaving everything you know for what you don't. What you trust to supply your needs for that which may or may not give anything at all. It means walking behind a man you may have only just heard of and away from a life you've known forever. You've breathed it, you've eaten it, and you've slept it. Can you—will you—trade the sound of waves lapping against aging wood, the caw of the gull, and the flap of caught fish for the sound of leather sandals slapping against the callused heels of a carpenter on an unlikely mission?

I open my eyes to an even more pressing question: where is *my* empty boat? Where is the evidence of what

Perhaps These Things Never Were

Perhaps these things never were.
Perhaps
I never rose with the dawn to the garden
To work it by the sweat of my brow?

Perhaps, in the long, blazing harvest days,
High atop a wagon heavy with sheaves
I never raised my voice in song?

I never purified myself in the tranquil blue
And the innocence
Of my Kinneret...O my Kinneret.
Were you there, or did I dream a dream?

—Poetess and pioneer Rachel, who lived by the Sea of Galilee (the Kinneret), 1927.

(From "The Poetry of Rachel," 23rd edition, Dvir: 1972, p. 79, in Hebrew. Translation: Miriam Feinberg Vamosh)

I have been willing to leave behind for what I say I follow?

Or have I, in fact, remained with the boat, too afraid to venture from the water and the shoreline and the fishing? Can I—will I—listen for that slap of sandals and the call of the great Fisherman beckoning me toward what I don't know but what he knows so well? *Follow me,* he says, and I think, *Yes! I believe I will.*

What surprises the Sea of Galilee brings.

Some of the followers were together: Simon Peter, Thomas (called Didymus), Nathanael from Cana in Galilee, the two sons of Zebedee, and two other followers. Simon Peter said, "I am going out to fish." The others said, "We will go with you." So they went out and got into the boat. They fished that night but caught nothing. Early the next morning Jesus stood on the shore, but the followers did not know it was Jesus. Then he said to them, "Friends, did you catch any fish?" They answered, "No." He said, "Throw your net on the right side of the boat, and you will find some." So they did, and they caught so many fish they could not pull the net back into the boat. The follower whom Jesus loved said to Peter, "It is the Lord!" When Peter heard him say this, he wrapped his coat around himself. (Peter had taken his clothes off.) Then he jumped into the water. The other followers went to shore in the boat, dragging the net full of fish. They were not very far from shore, only about a hundred yards. When the followers stepped out of the boat and onto the shore, they saw a fire of hot coals. There were fish on the fire, and there was bread. Then Jesus said, "Bring some of the fish you just caught." Simon Peter went into the boat and pulled the net to the shore. It was full of big fish, one hundred fifty-three in all, but even though there were so many, the net did not tear. Jesus said to them, "Come and eat." None of the followers dared ask him, "Who are you?" because they knew it was the Lord. When they finished eating, Jesus said to Simon Peter, "Simon son of John do you love me more than these?"

John 21:2–12, 15a

The Chapel of Peter's Primacy

*The Chapel of Peter's Primacy, built on a rocky outcropping
that was a fishermen's pier in ancient times.*

Did You Know?

he Galilee sunlight filters through the stained glass windows in the chapel of Peter's Primacy, daubing the massive bedrock around which the apse is built with splashes of warm color. Outside of this church, built in 1934 over the ancient rock and maintained, like many other holy sites around the lake, by the Franciscans, another part of that rock was carved by an ancient stonemason into a staircase. Once it led down to the water, and in years of good rainfall, when the Sea of Galilee is high, it may still do so. Fishing boats used to cast off from here, one of about fifteen small harbors uncovered around the shores.

This area, just to the east of the Church of the Multiplication of Loaves and Fishes, contains some of the seven springs of Tabgha. These mineral springs were ec-onomically important to the fishermen of Jesus' day; St. Peter's Fish or *tilapia,* a tropical breed that was their mainstay, were attracted to their warmth. To this day, as you sit quietly on the shoreline, you will see them churning the waters in their feeding frenzy.

The Gospels mention two miraculous catches of fish, both of which scholars picture happening right here. One, in Luke 5:1–7, occurred at the beginning of Jesus' Galilee ministry. The other, after the resurrection, was followed by Jesus' instruction to Peter: *Feed my sheep* (John 21:17). That charge is behind this site's name: "Peter's Primacy."

An understanding of the nets used in Jesus' day can help us picture the story in John as it took place here. The fishermen were using a trammel net, the only type

A feeding frenzy in the Sea of Galilee near the Chapel of Peter's Primacy. The warm water of the nearby springs made this prime fishing grounds, then and now.

The rocky outcropping outside forms part of the altar inside the Chapel of Peter's Primacy. The rock is also known as Mensa Christi, the "table of Christ" as tradition marks this as the spot where Jesus prepared fish for the disciples (John 21:9-13).

of ancient net still used today. It is made in sections as long as thirty-five yards and has three layers held together by a floating top rope and a weighted bottom rope. Fish come in through the larger meshes of the outer net, and get caught in the inner net. Releasing them was painstaking work that would be done in the morning, following a night of fishing. Then came the day-long repairs of the nets. The "nets" (plural) we read about in the Gospels (Mark 1:19; Matthew 4:21; Luke 5:2) would have been of the trammel type and were operated, then as now, by a team.

Jesus asks Peter to bring the fish he had caught. Peter does not bring these fish from the trammel net in the boat, where they would still have been entangled and which he could have never handled alone (John 21:11). Rather, it seems he was hauling a smaller net over to Jesus on the shore. The cast net was round, parachute like, and could be thrown from the side of the boat or the shallows.[1] Peter hauled in 153 large fish—not much for a trammel net, but an amazing amount for one man to carry in a cast net, unless that man was the utterly devoted Peter.

---

1 Mendel Nun. *The Sea of Galilee and its Fishermen in the New Testament* (Kibbutz Ein Gev: 1989), 23.

 riends! Haven't you any fish?"

Standing in the bay at Peter's Primacy, looking out over the Sea of Galilee as it laps its way toward shore, and watching the fishermen as they cast their nets over the sides of their boats, it's easy to hear the voice of the Lord calling out to the disciples who had decided to forsake the call for the catch. I stand with my feet braced, my hands on my hips. I close my eyes and—this time—witness the scene as it was then. Early morning. A few fishermen, near-naked as was the custom, slowly making their way toward the shore in a boat that had seen better days. And nights. Nets empty, their heads are down. *Can't we even get* this *right?* they wonder.

But Jesus, perhaps standing where I am now—is smiling. He knows the truth. He knows exactly how many fish the men have caught in their entire night's work. None.

"Friends!" he calls out. "Haven't you any fish?" Indeed, he knows the truth. What a joke to say, "*Haven't* you" meaning, "Did you really think you could go back to *this* kind of fishing?"

They admit they have not.

I open my eyes; my thoughts interrupted by what sounds like water rushing over the side of a cliff. I look to the right and see fish, teeming near the shore's edge.

I inch my way to the shore and watch until they settle down, then begin in their frenzy again as though to say, "Here we are! Catch!"

Throw your net on the right side of the boat, Jesus calls out. He must have seen what I am seeing now. One hundred fifty-three fish are hauled in. *It is the Lord!* John calls out.

I am wondering what it was in Jesus' demeanor that caused John to recognize him. Something in his stance? In the way he held his head when he spoke? The sunrise casting light and shadow in such a way as to be no mistaking him? Why did Peter throw his outer garment on? Did he think a simple piece of cloth would hide the nakedness of his betrayal? Then run *to* him? I think, as I stand here, I may have dove into the water and prayed the sea would take me to my eternal rest.

But run to Jesus, Peter did.

I climb over a low wall of aging rock and, alone, sit upon one of the stones in the shallow water. The fish are closer to me now; the water tickles my bare feet and soaks the hem of my jeans. In a strange way, I want to become one of those fish. I want to be hauled into a net and brought to Jesus and served up for breakfast.

Another sound startles me, and I look over my shoulder. A lone fish—large and dark—is slipping over the rocks directly behind me, heading toward the others. I watch as he joins them, and becomes one of a multitude.

Right: Ancient steps to a fishermen's dock ascend from the Sea of Galilee outside the Chapel of Peter's Primacy. Just above this reminder is the rock where, tradition states, Jesus stood as he called out to the disciples.

Left page: The setting sun illuminates the still waters at the Cove of the Sower on the northern shore of the Sea of Galilee.

When Jesus came to the area of Caesarea Philippi, he asked his followers, "Who do people say the Son of Man is?" They answered, "Some say you are John the Baptist. Others say you are Elijah, and still others say you are Jeremiah or one of the prophets." Then Jesus asked them, "And who do you say I am?" Simon Peter answered, "You are the Christ, the Son of the living God." Jesus answered, "You are blessed, Simon son of Jonah, because no person taught you that. My Father in heaven showed you who I am. So I tell you, you are Peter. On this rock I will build my church, and the power of death will not be able to defeat it.

Matthew 16:13–18

Caesarea Philippi

These niches were carved in the mid-first century AD. The Greek inscription below the upper niche, in which a statue of the wood-nymph Echo would have stood, reads: "The priest Victor, son of Lysimachos dedicated this goddess to the god Pan, lover of Echo."

Did You Know?

hen Canaan was divided among the tribes of Israel, what the New Testament calls Caesarea Philippi and what is now called Banias fell within the territory allotted to the tribe of Manassah. Nearly a millennium later, after the conquest of Alexander the Great in 332 BC, the allure of the spring and river, nestled in rich vegetation, led the Greeks to build a temple here to Pan—their half-goat, half-man deity who symbolized nature. They called the place Paneas after the name of the deity.

At the end of the first century BC, the Romans annexed Paneas to the kingdom of Herod the Great. Flavius Josephus tells us that Herod built a temple close to the springs and dedicated it to his patron, the Roman emperor Augustus. After Herod's death, his kingdom was divided among his three sons. Philip, the half-brother of Herod Antipas (Luke 3:19), made Paneas the capital of his kingdom in 2 BC, renaming it Caesarea Philippi. Herod's great-grandson, Agrippa II, later adorned the city with a palace and temples that are today mere shadows and whispers.

In the time of Herod Philip, worshippers of Pan once passed through a splendid gateway to an imposing temple that abutted a cave. The gate and the building are gone, but the cave into which the spring waters once welled and the worshippers threw in sacrificial goats can still be seen.

With the rise of Christianity during the Byzantine period (the beginning of the fourth century AD), the temples were abandoned and the city flourished. The

Left: *A sparkling cascade at the Banias River, the headwaters of the Jordan, at Caesarea Philippi.*

Right page: *The Banias waterfall.*

church fathers identified Paneas not only with Caesarea Philippi, but also as the place where Jesus healed the "woman who had been subject to bleeding" (Matthew 9:20 NIV; Mark 5:25 NIV; Luke 8:43 NIV). In gratitude for her healing, legend says the woman placed a statue of Jesus at the door of her house. No one knows what happened to the figure; it was believed to have been on display in one of the rooms of a Byzantine church that supplanted the pagan temple.

The Banias River, which emerges below the ruins, has its origin in snowmelt from Mount Hermon to the north. From Hermon, the river flows south, joined on the way by two other streams, the Dan and the Hatzbani, to become the Jordan River and go on to fill the Sea of Galilee. The stream banks are wild and beautiful, lined with poplar, willow, holy bramble, terebinth, laurel, and oak. Rock hyrax, the biblical coney, suns itself on the rocks, and at night wild boar, golden jackals, and beech martens roam the ridges. Rock doves make their nests in clefts in the spring cave; kestrels and blue rock thrush swoop and soar among the ruins.

Up the hill from the ancient remains is a site called Nebi Khader. The name means "the green one"; the Druze faith identifies him with Elijah the prophet. Elijah's connection with Banias is no coincidence: like these green surroundings, Elijah never died. And in another flourishing place, Mount Carmel, Elijah, too, faced the challenge of false gods and overcame them.

I am surrounded by oddity: the rushing water is running crystal clear and slipping over algae-covered rocks like melting icicles hanging off barren limbs after a winter's storm. The sun blazing from its noontime location plays coolly among the foliage and entices a coney to come out and watch from above the rocks. Against the deep blue of the sky, he appears the same color as the boulders around him, and had I blinked, I would have lost the joy of seeing him there.

There is strangeness here, this place of both pagan worship and godly aspirations. To be more like him, we must first know who he is, if for no one else but ourselves. Even drawing near to the place in the face of the cliff near where Herod's great white palace once stood

> **I** think this is a perfect place to come in our journey. Looking beyond the obvious, it is the place where the river flows and Peter declared his understanding not only of who Jesus is, but who he was to him.

and a gaping cave now opens its mouth as though in horror at the pagan sacrifices that took place here, I am reminded of who Herod thought he was, who Caesar believed he was, and who Philip established himself as.

Now nothing remains. Nothing, that is, save tourists and visitors and conies playing peekaboo among the rocks. And a grotto that once accepted the sacrifice of goats. I approach it, but I don't get too close. There is something still so very evil here. A presence, perhaps.

A memory. The fearful bleating. "The gates of hell" is an accurate description. On either side of the grotto are niches where statues of the gods once stood proudly overlooking the debauchery. Flesh and blood sacrificed to cold stone. I shiver, even in the warm sunlight.

Even so, I think this is a perfect place to come in our journey. Looking beyond the obvious, it is the place where the river flows and Peter declared his understanding not only of who Jesus is, but who he was to him. Had I blinked, I might have missed it.

I step over to the ruins of the worship center and look over to the landscape beyond. It is interesting that Jesus led his disciples to this region, I think. They were not there by happenstance. They were there by his designation. Perhaps his question to them, *Who do you say I am?* was spoken near where I am standing now, in the shadow of the shrine. The disciples' answer addressed who *others* said Jesus was. But Jesus asked them a more poignant question. More personal, in fact. "What about *you*?"

Peter knew.

Blessed are you, Simon.

I stoop down and pick up a stone, a tiny portion of the hulk behind me, and balance it in the palm of my hand. *And now you are "the rock." I will build my church on it and the gates of hell will not defeat it.*

Boys who play "Army" become men, I think, and still they talk of war. But this is spiritual warfare. The battle which began that day continues on, and even I am one of its soldiers. I stand, my shoulders arched back, and toss the stone to the ground.

The war goes on.

The Banias River overcomes a basalt-boulder slalom on its way to join the Jordan.

169

$\mathcal{A}$ man named Job lived
in the land of Uz. He was an
honest and innocent man; he
honored God and stayed away
from evil. Job had seven sons
and three daughters. He owned
seven thousand sheep, three
thousand camels, five hundred
teams of oxen, and five hundred
female donkeys. He also had a
large number of servants. He
was the greatest man among
all the people of the East.

Job 1:1–3

Ein Ayub

The warm waters of Ein Ayub, the spring of Job, burst into the Sea of Galilee.

O n the eastern reaches of the Cove of the Sower on the northern coast of the Sea of Galilee is one of the seven warm springs of Tabgha known as *Ein Ayub*, "the Spring of Job."

The name Job is spelled and pronounced very similarly in the sister languages of Hebrew and Arabic. In Hebrew it is *Iyov,* and in Arabic *Ayub*. The word for spring, one of the most important in both of these desert-born languages, is exactly the same. Arabic sacred literature and folklore share many themes with the Hebrew Bible, among them, a great interest in the trials and tribulations of Job.

Before the Spring of Job spills into the Sea of Galilee, it wells up as a pool inside a one-story, conical, roofless tower built of rough-hewn, black, basalt stones. Steps, in the form of protruding blocks, circle up to the top of the tower from the outside and down into the water from the inside. No one can say for sure when it was built. The legend recorded below, probably for the first time anywhere in English, is told by H'sein el Heib of the el Heib Bedouin tribe and director of Hazor National Park. Mr. el Heib was born in 1949 in a tent in the Hula Valley. He recalls coming down to the Spring of Job with his grandmother as a child, when he was a shepherd.

Left: *A giant acacia tree thrives near the spring of Job.*

Left page: *The morning sun's rays reach out from behind the clouds to touch the lake.*

The water was believed to have healing power, he says, and the tower was built around the pool to protect the modesty of the women, who would bathe there to cure their ills. Mr. el Heib goes on with the story:

Job was a prophet and a good man. God wanted to boast to Satan about Job's faithfulness, and so he took everything away from Job until there was nothing left but his body. He then caused him to have leprosy. The disease even reached Job's tongue. Job said to God, "If my tongue dies, how can I praise you?" And so God showed Job the spring that is now called Ein Ayub. This God did by having two doves splash in the water. Some of the water touched Job and healed him.

Meanwhile, Job's wife, whose name was Rahma ["mercy"] had no food because of the disasters that had struck them. A man said to her, "Sell me your braid, and I will give you food." And she did.

She then went to look for Job to give him food and found him at the spring. He was healthy, and so she did not recognize him. He insisted he was her husband, and showed her a birthmark on his shoulder to prove it. "But where is your hair?" Job asked.

"I sold it to get us food," she answered.

Job was very angry and took an oath to beat her one hundred times. But God said to Job, "You should not strike your wife. But since you took an oath, you should take one hundred soft sheaves of wheat and tap her once, and you will have fulfilled your oath."

Few know this story of the Ein Ayub. But in this legend of its healing waters, ancient and sacred memories reside.

arly morning. Clouds hang thick over the sea. The sun has yet to peek through, and there is a gray wash over the world. Water beckons. It lies over Galilee like a sheet over a sleeping child, moving only with the rhythmic breathing of the earth. There is no sound except the occasional caw of a bird.

We make our way down to the water, where misty light becomes more pronounced and rushing water sounds more intense. Water gushes from the side of the cove, and young men make small talk as they sit on a cluster of boulders. I note their yarmulkes and sandaled feet. "Jesus and the disciples," my friend whispers, nudging me. And I laugh.

And then we are there. A place, according to tradition, of healing. A place where Job—racked by a pain no man should ever endure—meets God in clear water.

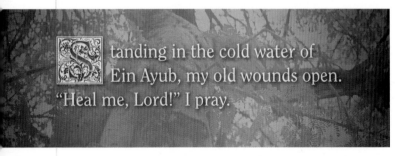

tanding in the cold water of Ein Ayub, my old wounds open. "Heal me, Lord!" I pray.

I stand motionless, remembering his story. A man who had it all: riches untold, sons and daughters, health in good measure, and a wife who loved him. Or so I imagine.

And then it was gone.

Wealth, children, health. The only thing left to him was his wife. In some cases this is a good thing; in some cases, not so much.

The world turns brighter around me. I look over my shoulder at the sea and watch clouds dissipate and rays of sunlight shoot down. The world is now truly awake. I slip off my shoes. It seems the right thing to do now. To do *here*.

I am wading in Job's healing waters, and I am feeling something more intense than I'd expected. A bittersweet memory pushes its way forward. I thought I'd forgotten it completely, erased it from the annals of my mind. But it comes, and it settles heavy inside.

Like Job, I have gained and lost. Not my children—blessedly no! But my worldly possessions, yes. Stolen by greed. Like Job, I have been sick. Not in the "I have a cold" way, but in the way that forces its victim to doctors and laboratories and to a weakness beyond belief. I have feared death and, more than death, the not knowing why.

Job, the Bible says, took pottery shards and scraped his wounds. Standing in the cold water of Ein Ayub, my old wounds open. "Heal me, Lord!" I pray. "Heal me as you healed Job. Wash my sores out to sea."

And he does.

It is later. I stand in the presence of my friend—a Jew—and a humble man—a Muslim. I listen enraptured as he recounts a story passed down from one generation to another until it was told to him. He speaks it in Hebrew; Miriam translates to English, and I strain to hear her over the baritone of his voice. I know this is a special moment in my life, but at first I don't know why.

And then, I do.

We have more in common, I realize, than we have differences . . . if we listen.

And so, I pray a new prayer: *Lord, heal this land.*

Cormorants resting on a branch at the Sea of Galilee shore near Ein Ayub.

lijah went before the people and said, "How long will you waver between two opinions? If the LORD is God, follow him; but if Baal is God, follow him." But the people said nothing. Then Elijah said to them, "I am the only one of the LORD's prophets left, but Baal has four hundred and fifty prophets. Get two bulls for us. Let them choose one for themselves, and let them cut it into pieces and put it on the wood but not set fire to it. I will prepare the other bull and put it on the wood but not set fire to it. Then you call on the name of your god, and I will call on the name of the LORD. The god who answers by fire—he is God." Elijah said to the prophets of Baal, "Choose one of the bulls and prepare it first. Call on the name of your god, but do not light the fire." So they took the bull given them and prepared it. Then they called on the name of Baal from morning till noon. But there was no response; no one answered. And they danced around the altar they had made. At noon Elijah began to taunt them. "Shout louder!" he said. "Surely he is a god! Perhaps he is deep in thought, or busy, or traveling. Maybe he is sleeping and must be awakened." So they shouted louder and slashed themselves with swords and spears, as was their custom, until their blood flowed. Midday passed, and they continued their frantic prophesying until the time for the evening sacrifice. But there was no response, no one answered, no one paid attention. Elijah took twelve stones, one for each of the tribes descended from Jacob, to whom the word of the LORD had come, saying, "Your name shall be Israel." With the stones he built an altar in the name of the LORD, and he dug a trench around it large enough to hold two seahs of seed. He arranged the wood, cut the bull into pieces and laid it on the wood. Then he said to them, "Fill four large jars with water and pour it on the offering and on the wood." The water ran down around the altar and even filled the trench. Elijah stepped forward and prayed: "O LORD, God of Abraham, Isaac and Israel, let it be known today that you are God in Israel and that I am your servant and have done all these things at your command. Answer me, O LORD, answer me, so these people will know that you, O LORD, are God, and that you are turning their hearts back again." Then the fire of the LORD fell and burned up the sacrifice, the wood, the stones and the soil, and also licked up the water in the trench. When all the people saw this, they fell prostrate and cried, "The LORD—he is God! The LORD—he is God!"

Excerpted from 1 Kings 18:21–39 NIV

Mount Carmel

A view of the Jezreel Valley from Mount Carmel, with Mount Gilboa in the distance.

he prophet Elijah was a one-man divine commando force, who had no problem bringing the battle for the Lord to the enemy's gates. When he declared war on a couple of Canaanite gods, Baal and Asherah (1 Kings 18:19), he did not go to the palace to confront Ahab's Phoenician wife, Jezebel, who had encouraged the worship of the pagan gods. Nor did he call Jezebel's priests and prophets to the desert he knew well, where the uncompromising surroundings proclaimed the oneness of God and out of which the Israelites brought this faith to the Promised Land.

Instead, Elijah went to Mount Carmel, whose name means "God's vineyard." Carmel is a thirty-five-mile long range of rolling limestone hills rising suddenly to about 1,500 feet above the northern Plain of Sharon and jutting straight into the sea from an otherwise straight coastline, like the prow of a ship plowing into the sea.

When rain clouds form over the Mediterranean and begin to move inland, Mount Carmel is the first place they make landfall. When they drop their rain, they make this range the greenest area for miles around. Oak, terebinth, and carob groves

Left: These blackened limestone boulders on Mount Carmel at Mukhraka, which means "burned," do indeed seem scorched, as by "the fire of the Lord" (1 Kings 18:38 NIV).

Right page: A rocky sanctuary on Mount Carmel near the Carmelite Monastery is a tranquil place to contemplate the fiery tale of Elijah's stand-off with the prophets of Ba'al, which tradition ascribes to this very site.

flourish here year-round. They sink their roots deep among the limestone outcroppings, some sharp enough to tear a hole in a Levite's cloak or Levi's jeans. The rocks and the trees are shelter and shade for gazelles, deer, foxes, porcupines, and other mammals, raptors, and songbirds. Carpets of wildflowers roll out in winter. Fertile ground indeed for swelling the ranks of the worshippers of a god they believed brought them that rain, Baal, and his consort, Asherah, whom they were sure they could count on for healthy and numerous offspring.

It's not difficult to imagine Jezebel, sailing down the coast from her father's kingdom in Phoenicia, with the priests and prophets of the one God whose faith she would challenge. Perhaps she landed right on the Carmel coast, at the port of Dor, placing a jeweled sandal on the quay and lifting her eyes to the mountain as she planned her conquest. Many shrines to Asherah, who is

among those false gods associated with trees, must have gone up on these wooded slopes in Jezebel's time.

What drew Elijah to Carmel? Drought. For seven years, no clouds had formed over the sea and no rain had come to Carmel, or anywhere else in the land. That meant one thing: God was angry that the people had bought the lie of idolatry.

Elijah, God's zealous warrior, called the prophets of Baal and Asherah to a contest on their own "turf," fertile Mount Carmel, challenging them to see who could bring down purifying fire from heaven. The fire did fall, at the pleasure of the one God, and consumed even the rocks and the soil. Wandering among those rocks today, you can see some that are mysteriously blackened, almost as if the righteous fire had fallen right here.

This was God's vineyard, not Baal's, and not Asherah's. And on that fateful day, Elijah proved it.

y heartbeat increases its pace with each step I take. Along the way, I stop—three times. Like a runner at the end of his race, I brace the palms of my hands on my thighs and wait for my breathing to return to something akin to normal. Unlike the runner, I have not crossed the finish line; I still have half a mountain to climb . . . and half a mind to return to where I started.

I am climbing Mount Carmel.

We arrive at the gates of the Carmelite monastery at Mukhraka, but bypass it altogether. I am anxious to look out over the vista below, a stone's throw away. When I reach my destination, I know the climb and the bypass have been worth it. I can see forever.

The land where time has played so much of her drama is right before me. I dart from one viewing place to the other until I feel a frenzy coming over me, perhaps such as the one that drove a people—the prophets of

of them. I touch them. They are rough, and I draw my hand back as though burned. I look up. The clouds glide overhead, and the sky—remarkable and blue—seems to be just beyond my reach, but no further.

Call on the name of your god! I hear the old man shout. *Shout louder!*

My breathing increases, though I've done nothing to warrant it. I spin around at the sound of the wind slipping through the trees. They hold a memory, I think, of unimaginable angst and glory. *Shout louder! Shout louder!*

Blood splatters across the face and chest of the great prophet. Deranged cries of prophecy to Baal burst from the mouths of the people, and their god has not listened. He has not heard. Elijah has had enough.

Bring the bull! Lay the wood! Pour the water!

My foot slips on a muddy patch of ground, and I sink down, the top of my thigh grazing one of the boulders deeply buried in the mountain. I bring my knees to my chest and look up again. A white, shredded cloud dances overhead, and a warm breeze combs my hair from my face.

I look out. Through the trees I see the patchwork of the Jezreel and the rise of Moreh. Surrounded by so much, I am alone here. Totally alone. Yet, I feel something . . . a Presence, perhaps . . . or the memory of one. I place my forehead on my knees and begin to weep.

> I look out. Through the trees I see the patchwork of the Jezreel and the rise of Moreh. Surrounded by so much, I am alone here. Totally alone. Yet, I feel something . . . a Presence, perhaps . . . or the memory of one.

Baal—to slash themselves with knives. This is the place where, in an effort to prove their lack of faith in the one true God and be justified by faith in *any* god, people allowed themselves to be foolhardy.

I step over to the cluster of large stones. They look angry. Dark, in spite of the flora and foliage growing out

A God, *my God.* so powerful to send his flames down to this place because of a man who'd had enough of idolatry. My God, who heard through the maniacal ravings a single prayer.

The Lord, I whisper in the glory. *He is God!*

A trail among the oaks at Mukhraka near the monastery on Mount Carmel.

181

Later Herod moved from Judea and went to the city of Caesarea, where he stayed. Herod was very angry with the people of Tyre and Sidon, but the people of those cities all came in a group to him. After convincing Blastus, the king's personal servant, to be on their side, they asked Herod for peace, because their country got its food from his country. On a chosen day Herod put on his royal robes, sat on his throne, and made a speech to the people. They shouted, "This is the voice of a god, not a human!" Because Herod did not give the glory to God, an angel of the Lord immediately caused him to become sick, and he was eaten by worms and died. God's message continued to spread and reach people.

Acts 12:19b–24

Caesarea Maritima

A Roman aqueduct that carried spring water to Caesarea fights conquest by the sand.

A view of the Roman hippodrome at Caesarea, with the palace of Herod and Pontius Pilate in the foreground and Crusader ruins in the distance.

Tyre, Ptolemais, Caesarea. The list in Acts of these fabled Holy Land coastal cities on Paul's missionary journey reads like an ancient Roman mariner's log. And for good reason: these last stages on Paul's journeys contained stops familiar to every sailor who crossed the Mediterranean from Italy. Ships made their way along the coast from north to south, trading at every port of call and seeking safe harbor every night. Hugging the coast allowed them to use familiar landmarks to navigate, restock supplies, and overcome treacherous east-west winds. At the busy port of Caesarea, they might offload wine from Rhodes, cloth from Damascus and Tyre, and luxury tableware from Italy. They would then reload their ships with perfumes like balsam and spices like the famed frankincense and myrrh from the deserts of the east. The marketplace of Caesarea was the world's meeting place for Jews, Samaritans, Greek and Roman pagans, Arabs, and even silk traders from India and China.

Rome took the tax revenues it accrued in Caesarea very seriously and protected its interests by stationing loyal Italian soldiers there. During Peter's time, their commander was the centurion, Cornelius, whose encounter with Peter changed the history of Christianity.

Caesarea was the queen of the coast—the largest Roman port in the eastern Mediterranean. It took Herod the Great some twelve years to build the city as a showcase for his Roman overlords, complete with a stadium where fifteen thousand spectators cheered charioteers; a theater where bawdy comedies were staged; villas, bath-houses, and fountains for its twelve thousand residents; and a gigantic temple to Emperor Augustus. Most amazing of all was its harbor—1,800 feet long and 160 feet wide—perched on massive walls sunken to the sea bed, and a huge lighthouse with an ever-burning beacon to guide the ships to shore.

And yet, only one hundred years after he built it, Caesarea lay in ruin, crushed, some scholars believe, by a tsunami following the eruption of Mount Vesuvius in Italy in AD 79. Caesarea rose again after Christianity overcame paganism. Archaeologists found one building used as a tax bureau, with a quote on a mosaic floor from Romans 13:3 reminding citizens to "do what is right"— a not-so-gentle reminder to people to obey authority and pay their taxes!

It is ironic that Caesarea, which in the days of Herod, Peter and Paul was perhaps the most materialistic and pagan city in the Holy Land, was also the home of one of the earliest Christian communities. What better place for Peter, years before, to have opened the way for the first Gentiles to come to the one God and for the followers of Jesus to impart their message to people from every land? In fact, if ever there was a place for a message to go out to the world, Caesarea was it.

Right: At Caesarea, a cat commands ruins where Crusaders once stood their ground.

Left: Water, water everywhere: A view of the Mediterranean through one of the arches of the Roman aqueduct that carried spring water to Caesarea.

usk arrives.

Caesarea Maritima's modern shop owners are pulling blinds, locking doors, and turning out lights. Tomorrow will bring more shoppers who want a piece for a price. A few cafés remain open, dimly lit against the darkening pink and orange of the sky over the deep blue of the Great Sea. It rushes forward, sending frothy spray along the coastline and dancing around fishermen sporting vests and slick waders—men who seek life among drenched ruins.

The Roman aqueduct, a one-time source of water for a city built in honor of everything *but* God, stretches long in the pale sand of the Mediterranean, providing arched windows toward the ocean. It stands like a centurion in some places, like an old man in others. I step through it, allowing my fingers to brush against its stone. I scan the length of it; it seems to moan under the weight of time. Overhead, a movement. I look up and into the eyes of a stray cat peering down as if to ask, "Friend or foe?"

I smile, then I turn and head toward the Crusaders' fortress. Slipping under its arched doorways, we find ourselves in a gatehouse that feels like a setting in a Gothic novel. On the other side is an expanse of ruins that brags of the hunger of man and the power of God. It was at one time one man's dream and mankind's nightmare. It speaks of the brilliance of Herod and the maniacal repercussions of his command against Jew and Christian alike.

The sun drops lower, and we are in the vacant amphitheater. An iron replica of a horse-drawn chariot

Left: *Eerie iron steeds rear their heads in the Roman hippodrome to recall ancient chariot races.*

Right page: *Restored Roman pillars show where the originals once surrounded an open courtyard in Herod's Caesarea palace.*

stands as though forgotten on the stage. The horses—shoulders back, ears pointed, hooves prancing—point us toward the palace, or what remains of it. We continue to walk the length of Herod's dream, my Jewish friend and I, our footsteps echoing amid the haunted cries of untold numbers of Jews and Christians who died here for the entertainment of their Roman superiors.

We reach the hill just beyond the palace and sit at the edge of a cliff, the edge of a world, really. Below, as though angry at what happened here—Paul's imprisonment, the sport of the innocent pitted against ferocious animals, and the spectacle of man fighting against man until the bloody death of the weaker one—waves crash against all that is left. Stone once erected in haughty dedication to Caesar Augustus lies broken and breaking still.

In spite of it all, there is an energy here. It survived the rule of the Romans and rose on the prayers of the faithful. The stories of Cornelius, Philip, Philip's four daughters, and the Jews who stood faithful, shine against a backdrop of horror.

We head back from what ceased to be to what continues. We move silently—my Jewish friend and I—past the narrow seats of the amphitheater where crowds watched our ancestors martyred.

The ocean's breeze pushes us forward, and she speaks: "Look who is walking through whose ruins now."

From the Beginning to the End: Jerusalem!

_D_uring Elizabeth's sixth month of pregnancy, God sent the angel Gabriel to Nazareth, a town in Galilee, to a virgin. She was engaged to marry a man named Joseph from the family of David. Her name was Mary.

Mary got up and went quickly to a town in the hills of Judea. She came to Zechariah's house and greeted Elizabeth. When Elizabeth heard Mary's greeting, the unborn baby inside her jumped, and Elizabeth was filled with the Holy Spirit. She cried out in a loud voice, "God has blessed you more than any other woman, and he has blessed the baby to which you will give birth. Why has this good thing happened to me that the mother of my Lord comes to me? When I heard your voice, the baby inside me jumped with joy. You are blessed because you believed that what the Lord said to you would really happen." Then Mary said, "My soul praises the Lord; my heart rejoices in God my Savior, because he has shown his concern for his humble servant girl. From now on, all people will say that I am blessed, because the Powerful One has done great things for me. His name is holy. God will show his mercy forever and ever to those who worship and serve him. He has done mighty deeds by his power. He has scattered the people who are proud and think great things about themselves. He has brought down rulers from their thrones and raised up the humble. He has filled the hungry with good things and sent the rich away with nothing. He has helped his servant, the people of Israel, remembering to show them mercy as he promised to our ancestors, to Abraham and to his children forever." Mary stayed with Elizabeth for about three months and then returned home.

Luke 1: 26–27, 39–56

Ein Karem

Daisies and geraniums flourish in the shade of an olive tree on the path up to the Visitation Church sanctuary.

 icturesque stone houses dot the hillsides in the village of Ein Karem, the traditional "city of Judah" that was the birthplace of John the Baptist on the southern outskirts of Jerusalem. We leave the houses behind, heading up the hill where Christians built their churches a century and a half ago. Here also are the stone walls of terraces built by the ancient farmers who raised grapes here, giving the village its name, *Ein Karem*, "spring of the vineyard." The grapevines, too, are still there, climbing wildly over the terraces, clinging to fig and terebinth trees, still singing the Song of the Vineyard of Isaiah 5.

The Magnificat in more than forty languages adorns a wall of the Visitation Church courtyard.

Ein Karem is the heart of the region where John *grew up and became strong in spirit . . .* (Luke 1:80). But we are here to commemorate a time before John's birth, when Mary visited her kinswoman Elizabeth. We pass through the gateway between now and then, between the ordinary and the sacred, to the Church of the Visitation, which marks the site of that meeting. Before doing so, we take in the hills to the north, on one of which is the prophet Samuel's tomb, because we are here to pay homage to three women: the mother of Jesus, the mother of John, and the mother of Samuel—Hannah.

We open our Bibles to the Magnificat, Mary's exquisite poem of praise (Luke 1:46–55), and to Hannah's joyful song (1 Samuel 2:1–10). No other "classroom" could be more appropriate to make these verses our own than the cool of this hilltop chapel that marks Mary's encounter with Elizabeth.

As we read, we realize that both women recognized they were the personal recipients of divine favor. In Mary's words *My soul praises the Lord . . . because he has shown his concern for his humble servant girl.* (Luke 1:46, 48). Hannah said, *My heart rejoices in the LORD; my horn is exalted in the LORD* (1 Samuel 2:1 NKJV).

We understand that both women lived by the faith that God cares for vulnerable groups, the hungry and the barren. As Mary sang it: *He has filled the hungry with good things* (Luke 1:53). And Hannah knew: *People who were hungry are hungry no more. The woman who could not have children now has seven.* (1 Samuel 2:5).

Both women recognized that divine actions are bestowed to honor the promise to Israel's ancestors and to all their descendants. Mary chanted: *As he promised to our ancestors, to Abraham and to his children forever* (Luke 1:55). Hannah sang: *He lets the poor sit with princes and receive a throne of honor* (1 Samuel 2:8).[1]

Perhaps for us, who come here seeking both to emulate these women and to build bridges of biblical heritage, the link they perceived through the generations, which we represent and are privileged to pass on, is the most significant lesson of them all.

---

1 With thanks for inspiration to Sister Joan Cook's book *Hannah's Desire, God's Design. Journal for the Study of the Old Testament Supplement Series 282* (Sheffield: Sheffield Academic Press, 1999).

A traditional painting of Mary and Elizabeth in the chapel beneath the Visitation Church.

The slopes and hills leading to Jerusalem's Ein Karem are steeper than they appear at first glance. I am forced to stop several times as we hoof our way toward the Church of the Visitation. There is a low wall to my right, perfect for resting, for catching my breath, and for looking at the valley below. Rising high above the homes and businesses is the steeple of the Church of Saint John the Baptist, noted for its cross and its clock. Time, it reminds me, is ticking.

I press my hand against my chest at the magnitude of what is being featured here.

Three months more, and the aging Elizabeth will give birth.

I shift my gaze to look over my right shoulder. We are more than a hundred miles from Nazareth. Thirty-three years from another hill in Jerusalem.

I push myself from the wall. Across the narrow roadway a higher wall casts shade, and I think it would be cooler there. I slip into its shadow and continue my ascent. I think about Mary making this same trek; the shade from the olive trees her only respite. I wonder where, along the way, the Holy Spirit visited her, empowered her with a life to be born of her womb. How could someone so young comprehend such things?

We finally arrive at the Church of the Visitation, pass through its wrought iron gates, and enter into a courtyard of stone and statue and plaques in more than forty languages all declaring the same words: *My soul magnifies the Lord!*

Before them is a stone representation of the two kinswomen, one with a swollen belly. What manner of woman was this Elizabeth, I wonder. Perhaps even as she wondered.

But who am I that the mother of my Lord should come to me?

Above the arches of the breezeway leading to the door of the church is a magnificent mosaic of a young girl arriving on a donkey. I smile up at it; having now climbed to this location, I imagine it would have been an easier method of travel than by foot.

Inside the sanctuary are equally impressive murals, rich in color and emotion. They draw me farther into the building and further back in time. I press my hand against my chest at the magnitude of what is being featured here.

My soul . . .

I slip into a corner. My friend and I stand here as Elizabeth and Mary might have done millennia ago. Two women. One heavenly Father. One binding Holy Spirit.

She hands me a Bible, turned already to Luke 1. "Read it," she says. "Read it aloud."

My eyes scan the words on the page; they blur through my tears. I wonder, *What manner of girl was this who—as her ancestor Hannah had done so long before her—sang this song?*

These were her thoughts, too, I see. Mary knew what I *should* know: there is a fine line between weakness and power. Humble servant girl that she was, she became the most revered woman of all time. Not so much because she gave birth, but because she was willing to climb difficult hills with God and allow him to do great things through her.

A contemporary bronze Elizabeth and Mary clasp hands in the garden of the Visitation Church.

*T*hen the Spirit led Jesus into the desert to be tempted by the devil. Jesus fasted for forty days and nights. After this, he was very hungry. The devil came to Jesus to tempt him, saying, "If you are the Son of God, tell these rocks to become bread." Jesus answered, "It is written in the Scriptures, 'A person lives not on bread alone, but by everything God says.'" Then the devil led Jesus to the holy city of Jerusalem and put him on a high place of the Temple. The devil said, "If you are the Son of God, jump down, because it is written in the Scriptures: 'He has put his angels in charge of you. They will catch you in their hands so that you will not hit your foot on a rock.'" Jesus answered him, "It also says in the Scriptures, 'Do not test the Lord your God.'" Then the devil led Jesus to the top of a very high mountain and showed him all the kingdoms of the world and all their splendor. The devil said, "If you will bow down and worship me, I will give you all these things." Jesus said to the devil, "Go away from me, Satan! It is written in the Scriptures, 'You must worship the Lord your God and serve only him.'" So the devil left Jesus, and angels came and took care of him.

Matthew 4:1–11

The Pinnacle of the Temple

The Pinnacle of the Temple still towers over us at the southeastern corner of the Temple Mount.

ost of our attempts to come close to the buildings and streets that Jesus knew involve peering into holes at least ten feet into the ground, which archaeologists tell us was the level where life went on two thousand years ago. But in one amazing place in Jerusalem, you can look *up* at remains from Jesus' time. That place is the Pinnacle of the Temple.

The "Pinnacle of the Temple" (Matthew 4:5 NKJV; Luke 4:9 NKJV), where Jesus was tempted by the devil, is *ophel* in Hebrew. The Hebrew-English dictionary needs two words to properly explain that term: "fortified hill," which is exactly the way many modern translations render the term.

The Pinnacle of the Temple towers 120 feet high and is the southeastern corner of the outer wall of the Temple of Herod the Great, which the disciples thought no less than "magnificent" (Mark 13:1 NIV). Many of the building blocks hulking in the lower portion of this corner have regular margins carved around their edges. Herod did not invent this style, but it became his architectural insignia.

Despite the destruction of the Temple by the Romans, this corner, like the famed Western Wall, was not demolished. Many legends surround the survival of these walls, but the truth is, they were too colossal to succumb entirely to the Roman siege machines. It was more than a house of God: while those who came on pilgrimage here may have seen it as a stronghold of divine service, Herod also built it to serve as a stronghold against enemies real and imagined. That, to the Roman mind, was another very good reason to bring it down.

Southwest of the Pinnacle are the Southern Steps that once led into the Temple via the Gate Beautiful (Acts 3:2) where Peter healed a beggar. About one hundred feet to the north of the Pinnacle is "the seam," on either side of which the stones differ in size and workmanship. The section of the wall to the right of the seam dates from before the time of Jesus. Herod added the part on the left when he extended Mount Moriah to what has been calculated as approximately

---

wo brothers owned a field in Jerusalem. One had a wife and children while the other was a bachelor. They always shared their harvest equally, making two piles. But one year, the harvest was poor. The bachelor thought, "My brother has a wife and children to support." So in the middle of the night he secretly took wheat from his own pile and added it to his brother's. Meanwhile, the other brother said to his wife: "I have you and children, while my brother has no one. Let us secretly add to his portion from ours." Over several nights, the brother saw their piles were not decreasing. Keeping watch one night, they realized they were giving to each other. God chose the spot where two brothers acted selflessly to build the Temple, and so that place is blessed in all the earth.*

*Louis Ginzberg. "Legends of the Jews" Volume IV (57), online edition: www.philologos.org

A view of the Pinnacle from the Mount of Olives, showing, to its right, the seam that indicates Herod's addition to the Temple plaza.

It isn't easy to get a close look at the seam. A Muslim cemetery is here now, and political sensitivities being what they are, those of other religions cannot always come close to the others' deceased. The graves, many bearing still-fresh palm fronds carried by mourners, lie densely across the hill. They crowd around the now-locked Golden Gate, where tradition says the Messiah will enter Jerusalem, approximately in the middle of the 1,600-foot-long eastern wall.

Craning your neck, you can see where Herod's masonry ends and more ordinary building blocks that are "only" five hundred years old begin. Imagine you are back in Jesus' time, and stretch that wall skyward another 45 feet. The numbers help us to imagine the scene of Jesus' temptation, but they cannot do justice to the moment.

500 by 300 meters,[1] or approximately 1,615,000 square feet to bear the weight of the Temple, the largest building project in the Roman world.

A view of the Jewish cemetery on the Mount of Olives, sacred ground in which to await the coming of the Messiah.

---

1 Abraham Warszawski and Abraham Peretz, "Building the Temple." *Eretz* Magazine 46 (May–June 1996): 41.

've been staring at it off and on all morning. I've peered at it through the lofty pines as we descended Mount Zion. I've gazed at it over the walls of a garden called Gethsemane. I realize I am viewing the beginning of Jesus' ministry from the place where it ended.

Sort of.

Later in the morning, we are in my friend's car, zooming around the swaying curves in the roads around Jerusalem. Buses careen toward us, and I think they will topple over and into the Kidron Valley below. At times I think we will too. We slip into a parking spot, then my friend thinks better of it, and we are pulling out of it and into an overlook.

She stays with the car while I cross the road, darting between vehicles like Ms. Pac-Man maneuvering to avoid ghosts along the way. I reach the grassy knoll rolling between modern asphalt and ancient stone and slow my pace. I am approaching something bigger than I realized from the distance of Gethsemane.

At the base of the pinnacle, I look up. My neck cranes to the point of pain. My knees go weak at the thought of being at its top rather than its base. At some point, I sit in the damp grass. I allow my eyes to take in the magnitude of height.

It is tall.

Nothing is lost on me here. This was the place of temptation, the place of victory. I've been dancing between the two all morning when I took quick steps down the incline of Mount Zion. Had I gone too fast, I would have fallen face forward.

Left page: *A view of the Pinnacle from the Mount of Olives. The Dormition Church on Mount Zion is in the background.*

Below: *The Pinnacle of the Temple, rising above the part of the Kidron Valley known as the Valley of Jehosafat, studded with olive trees.*

When I was sheltered behind an iron gate in the Garden of Gethsemane, I took a moment to sit beneath a tree and ponder the magnitude of what took place there. It would have been so easy to have walked away that night two thousand years ago, to have turned away from the city walls of Jerusalem. Tempting, but no.

Even as the car slipped from one parking spot to another, I am mindful of how sometimes we need to just *move*. But, other times we're stuck in the middle of traffic, dodging cars like stray bullets. It would have been better to have stayed with the car.

Forty days and nights without food. Without water. Brought to what must have felt like a million miles from safety, Jesus stands being tempted by one who has been his nemesis forever.

"Jump. Come on; you can do it. They would never let you fall. Not now, not with your work being so close at hand. Isn't that what the Scriptures say? Jump."

I stand. *Do not test the Lord your God.*

Scripture for scripture. Sometimes, I think, you have to know your enemy as well as you know yourself.

The sound of cars brings me back to the present. I brush off my backside and turn toward the road and my friend who waits near her car. A glance toward the sun, now directly overhead, and my suspicions are confirmed. Temptations, for me, continue.

It is near noon, and I am hungry.

The Day of Unleavened Bread came when the Passover lambs had to be sacrificed. Jesus said to Peter and John, "Go and prepare the Passover meal for us to eat." They asked, "Where do you want us to prepare it?" Jesus said to them, "After you go into the city, a man carrying a jar of water will meet you. Follow him into the house that he enters, and tell the owner of the house, 'The Teacher says: Where is the guest room in which I may eat the Passover meal with my followers?' Then he will show you a large, furnished room upstairs. Prepare the Passover meal there." So Peter and John left and found everything as Jesus had said. And they prepared the Passover meal. When the time came, Jesus and the apostles were sitting at the table. He said to them, "I wanted very much to eat this Passover meal with you before I suffer. I will not eat another Passover meal until it is given its true meaning in the kingdom of God." Then Jesus took a cup, gave thanks, and said, "Take this cup and share it among yourselves. I will not drink again from the fruit of the vine until God's kingdom comes." Then Jesus took some bread, gave thanks, broke it, and gave it to the apostles, saying, "This is my body, which I am giving for you. Do this to remember me." In the same way, after supper, Jesus took the cup and said, "This cup is the new agreement that God makes with his people. This new agreement begins with my blood which is poured out for you."

Luke 22:7–20

The Upper Room

Pilgrims preparing for worship beneath the medieval arches in the Upper Room.

They certainly knew about arches in Roman times, but they didn't figure out how to make them pointed, like the ones in the Upper Room on Mount Zion, until many centuries later. They knew about writing, of course, but Arabic inscriptions like the ones that adorn the walls of this chamber, also known as the Room of the Last Supper or the Cenacle, were some eight hundred years away from coming into being. So how can this be the place where Jesus celebrated the Last Supper?

As visitors to Jerusalem know, to see anything that dates back to Jesus' time, you have to descend thirty feet below ground level, not go up a flight of stairs. The Room of the Last Supper we now visit dates from Crusader times, when the most important thing a Christian pilgrim could do was to get as close as possible to holy places, which were not always the historically accurate sites. That's how traditional sites are born. The Crusaders even left us evidence of their presence—a small, carved capital in a corner of the room depicts pelicans feeding their young, an ancient, rare, and powerful symbol of the Eucharist.

But the actual room of the Last Supper was in fact probably somewhere right below us. The three faithful tools that help us sleuth our way to this conclusion are the Gospels, of course, the Roman-Jewish historian Flavius Josephus, and archaeology.

The Essenes play an important role in this story. They were a group of men who believed in separating themselves from the Roman community, a lifestyle they saw as morally and ritually tainted, and awaiting the approaching End of Days. They were usually celibate and even had a different calendar than other Jews. The writings of Josephus Flavius and archaeological findings indicate that a group of Essenes apparently lived on Mount Zion.[1]

As Passover approached, Jesus knew he would soon be arrested. Jesus needed that Passover meal—whose symbolism in every aspect has made it one of the greatest educational tools of Jewish ritual life—to impart important truths. And so he may have chosen to celebrate with the Essenes, who, because of their differing calendar, celebrated Passover earlier in the week than other Jews. Preparations had to be clandestine; to find the locale, the disciples were to follow a man carrying a water jar (Mark 14:13; Luke 22:10). Carrying water was women's work, unless there were no women, and there were no female Essenes.

By the fourth century, speaking in tongues and the other events of Acts 2:1–41 were commemorated in the same location. Churches were built and destroyed on this site, reflecting the vicissitudes of Jerusalem's history, including a period of possession in the fifteenth century by Muslims.

And so, when Christians gather in this room, they can imagine the original site buried far below them under layers of rubble and mountains of faith. Their prayers here bring together what is above and what is below in more ways than one.

---

1 Josephus Flavius *Antiquities of the Jews* 15:373–379; Bargil Pixner, "Jerusalem's Essene Gateway: Where the Community Lived in Jesus' Time." *Biblical Archaeological Review* (May–June 1997). 66.

A contemporary sculpture of an olive tree now adorns the Room of the Last Supper.

I am surprised by many things in this cenacle, or dining hall, most of which is how detached I feel upon our arrival. I think perhaps it is due to the clusters of people about the large room, as though they have gathered to nibble at small but vital elements of history. Then, I find myself distracted by teens who have come with their teacher to learn more about *my* faith, which is so deeply rooted in *their* faith.

At first I wander about aimlessly, listening as my friend points out specific points of architecture within these walls. Pelicans, she says, pointing to the top of a column, are very symbolic to the Christian. "A reminder of the Eucharist," she says.

Funny, I think, *that she—a Jew—should know this, and not I.*

I move from the door leading out of the Room of the Last Supper and over to a short flight of stairs leading—seemingly—nowhere. Another group of teens—young men, mostly—have entered by that same door, and they are a bit rowdy. Someone shushes them, and—as teenage boys will do— they shush back. They giggle a bit, tickled by their own mirth.

I turn. Camera poised, I am struck by the window before me. It is like so many I've seen in cathedrals, and yet . . . *not*. Windows, I think, are for looking out *and* looking in.

Window see into more than just a room, I know. They see inside a soul as well. Then I think that to see inside my soul, I must look inside this room.

What do you see?

In spite of the lack of furnishings, I can imagine a low table and a gathering of men reclining around it in a room that was exactly as Jesus said it would be.

In a room much like this one, Jesus took the unleavened, pierced bread—the matza—in his hands and broke it. *This is my body.*

Four cups of wine—sanctification, judgment, redemption, praise—all partaken of. *This is my blood.*

Twelve men marked the words of the Teacher.

A reconstructed window dating from the 16th century, and an Arabic inscription recall days when the Cenacle was used as a mosque.

The unique capital in the Upper Room showing pelicans, an ancient Christian symbol.

like those spoken to Philip: *Don't you know me, Philip? Even after all this time?*

I return to the capital carved with pelicans. From somewhere comes the memory of the legend that a pelican will draw its own blood in sacrifice to provide for its young. I understand the symbolism now, and I reach up to touch the stone.

Don't you know me? I hear the whisper. *Even after all this time?*

The young men—the students—now shuffle out from the other side of the room; they've listen intently to *their* teacher. Perhaps, as they had earlier, the Twelve had shushed and chuckled.

For a moment.

I descend the steps and look to my right. There, under an archway, is a statue. A pruned olive tree, its branches budding. Like the window, it captivates me. *I am the vine; you are the branches.*

So many words spoken in the room this room represents. Denials predicted. Future sermon notes given. *Greater love has no man.* Strict commands expressed. Earnest prayers prayed. Encouragement passed along. *Don't let your hearts be troubled.* But none shakes me

This hymn, *Adoro te Devote*, attributed to St. Thomas Aquinas (1225–1274), contains a reference to the pelican as a symbol of Jesus in the following verse.

O thou our reminder of Christ crucified,
Living Bread, the life of us for whom he died,
Lend this life to me then: feed and feast my mind,
There be thou the sweetness man was meant to find.

Bring the tender tale true of the Pelican;
Bathe me, Jesu Lord, in what Thy bosom ran
Blood whereof a single drop has power to win
All the world forgiveness of its world of sin.

*(Translation, Gerald Manley Hopkins)
*www.seadoration.org/Hymns/adoro_te_devote.htm

Since it was almost time for David to die, he gave his son Solomon his last commands. David said, "My time to die is near. Be a good and strong leader. Obey the LORD your God. Follow him by obeying his demands, his commands, his laws, and his rules that are written in the teachings of Moses. If you do these things, you will be successful in all you do and wherever you go. And if you obey the LORD, he will keep the promise he made to me. He said: 'If your descendants live as I tell them and have complete faith in me, a man from your family will always be king over the people of Israel.'"

Then David died and was buried with his ancestors in Jerusalem. He had ruled over Israel forty years—seven years in Hebron and thirty-three years in Jerusalem.

1 Kings 2:1–4, 10–11

David's Tomb

An ancient arch frames two ultra-Orthodox men on their way in to David's Tomb.

No other holy site in this land embraces so many traditions—Jewish, Christian, and Muslim—as does the Tomb of King David. When prayers are said at the tomb today, they echo among walls that have over the centuries belonged to a synagogue, a church, and a mosque. The Room of the Last Supper is part of the same medieval structure and sits directly above the tomb. The most ordinary question is: how can this place, high on the hill above the city that David founded, be the tomb? After all, 1 Kings 2:10 says David was buried in the city of David. Did the reformer King Josiah erect a monument here to David after removing his bones from the city (2 Kings 23:16)? Was it here that Jews, returned from Babylonian captivity, paid homage to David (Nehemiah 3:16)? Was this the tomb Peter referred to as "with us today" in his sermon in the Upper Room (Acts 2:29)?

What we do know is that for at least one thousand years, the tomb has been marked here on Mount Zion, and over that millennium, poets have sung its praises, artists have drawn it, and penitents have made their pilgrimages to it.

What could resonate so powerfully in the hearts of so many, if not David's sheer humanity? David, whose name means "beloved," was never lost to God. David endured or succumbed to many temptations. Some, the Jewish sages say, came from nature: the impact on his character of his descent from the idol-worshipping Moabites is a popular topic in rabbinic literature. Others, from nurture: David's youthful victories were said to have given him such an overdose of self-confidence that he asked God to set bathing Bathsheba in his line of sight (2 Samuel 11:2) as a test![1]

David's complexities have given prayer at his tomb special significance in Jewish tradition. Many prayers seek divine protection for David's sake or entreat God for healing and spiritual strength for oneself or others. One beautiful tradition is to focus the mind and heart by praying portions of Psalm 119, which is alphabetical in Hebrew, by picking out the chapters that form the letters of the name of the individual in need. When the prayer is for a deceased loved one, prayer includes the verses under the letters spelling the word *neshamah* (soul).

Despite his failings, David is also the sweet singer of Israel, the traditional author of Psalms, the quintessential warrior and leader, and the founder of the eternal

---

1 Babylonian Talmud, Sanhedrin 104a

בשובה
את
שיבת ציון
היינו
כחולמים

לעילוי נשמות
אליהו בן יעקב הבקר ז"ל
אליהו גבריאל ז"ל

dynasty of the Messiah. In his multi-faceted character, perhaps he is a bit like Peter, another impetuous red-head (they say), whose denial of Jesus is marked by a church just a stone's throw from here and to whom reconciliation came at the Sea of Galilee.

In addition to the first words of Psalm 137:5, inscribed on the velvet covering are the words of one of the first songs every Jewish child learns, say it all: *David Melech Yisrael, Chai Vekayam*: "David, King of Israel, still lives."

Above: *A glass enclosed Torah scroll, donated to honor King David's final resting place, stands on the tomb marker in an ancient alcove.*

Left: *The* parochet, *or curtain, over the Holy Ark (containing Torah scrolls), embroidered with the opening words of Psalm 126.*

211

he entryway is near stifling; I stand heel-to-toe with the many. Lines of people from nations and faiths—Jews and Christians and Muslims—file in from the secluded courtyard belonging to a fourteenth-century Franciscan monastery. They stop for a photo-op at the large oak-framed cabinet—a Holy Ark holding Torah scrolls—its center draped in a deep velvet curtain, bordered with vines of petite flowers, adorned by a finely stitched crown, and scored in gold. The Hebrew, my friend whispers in my ear, reads, *When the Lord brought back the captivity of Zion, we were like those who dream.* It is, she tells me, from Psalm 126, one of the psalms of ascent.

The crowd moves on, ready to separate—men from women—before entering the tomb. But I stand back against the wall in front of the cabinet and contemplate the words. I am here, in Israel, because—in my own way—I have dared to dream and, out of the dreaming, dared to touch.

From beyond the walls, whispers of prayers mingle with the shuffling of feet and the mournful song of a man from somewhere I cannot see. It seems at times to come from before me, then from behind. I don't know. I only know that listening to the doleful rise and fall of the psalm stirs my heart as though I am sitting in a dimly lit theater, listening to an opera. "The sweet psalmist of Israel," I read somewhere. "As long as his words are sung, he will live on in the human hearts of man." My memory of the words may not be exact, but the sentiment is undeniable. Especially here. Especially now.

The crowd thins, and I seize my chance to be alone with the king. Not totally alone. A young woman, holding her child close, prays in earnest. She wraps her arms around him and draws him close to her, kissing him on his forehead, then runs her fingertips into his curly mop of hair in that way mothers do.

I sit in a small folding chair and think about David's final moments. Calling his son to his side, giving him final instructions in the way of fathers who are kings to sons who are about to be. I wonder if Solomon sat on his father's bed, took his father's seventy-year-old hand (a hand that held the lifeblood of countless others) in his twenty-year-old hand (a hand that would be known more for loving than warring). I wonder if Solomon ran his thumb over wrinkled age spots. If he wept. If tears slipped down his cheeks and onto the royal covers keeping the king warm.

"Be strong, my son. Be a man. Follow God. Keep his ways."

What measure of a man was David? I have seen the city of his birthplace, the valley where he fought, the caves where he hid, and now here. I think that it was his words to his son that were his height and breadth, this man who sought the

> erusalem, if I forget you,
> let my right hand lose its skill.
> Let my tongue stick to the roof of my mouth
> if I do not remember you,
> if I do not think about Jerusalem
> as my greatest joy.
>
> —Psalm 137:5–6

heart of God. I suppose what they say is true: after a man is gone, what matters most remains—the impression of his life on the history of humankind. *Then David rested with his fathers and was buried in the City of David* (1 Kings 2:10 NIV).

And I think: what will they say about me when I rest with my ancestors?

A young girl steeps herself the sacred text, her prayer book resting against King David's velvet-draped tomb marker.

David mustered the men who were with him and appointed over them commanders of thousands and commanders of hundreds. The king told the troops, "I myself will surely march out with you." But the men said, "You must not go out." The king answered, "I will do whatever seems best to you." So the king stood beside the gate while all the men marched out in units of hundreds and of thousands. The king commanded Joab, Abishai and Ittai, "Be gentle with the young man Absalom for my sake." The army of Israel was defeated by David's men, and the casualties that day were great—twenty thousand men.

Now Absalom happened to meet David's men. He was riding his mule, and as the mule went under the thick branches of a large oak, Absalom's head got caught in the tree. He was left hanging in midair, while the mule he was riding kept on going. When one of the men saw this, he told Joab, "I just saw Absalom hanging in an oak tree." Joab said to the man who had told him this, "What! You saw him? Why didn't you strike him to the ground right there? Then I would have had to give you ten shekels of silver and a warrior's belt." But the man replied, "Even if a thousand shekels were weighed out into my hands, I would not lift my hand against the king's son. Joab said, "I'm not going to wait like this for you." So he took three javelins in his hand and plunged them into Absalom's heart while Absalom was still alive in the oak tree.

[The troops] took Absalom, threw him into a big pit in the forest and piled up a large heap of rocks over him. Meanwhile, all the Israelites fled to their homes. During his lifetime Absalom had taken a pillar and erected it in the King's Valley as a monument to himself, for he thought, "I have no son to carry on the memory of my name." He named the pillar after himself, and it is called Absalom's Monument to this day.

While David was sitting between the inner and outer gates, the watchman went up to the roof of the gateway by the wall. As he looked out, he saw a man running alone. The watchman called out to the king and reported it. The king said, "If he is alone, he must have good news." And the man came closer and closer. . . . The king asked, "Is the young man Absalom safe?" . . . The Cushite replied, "May the enemies of my lord the king and all who rise up to harm you be like that young man." The king was shaken. He went up to the room over the gateway and wept. As he went, he said: "O my son Absalom! My son, my son Absalom! If only I had died instead of you—O Absalom, my son, my son!"

Excerpted from 2 Samuel 18 NIV

Kidron Valley

Landscape of kings, princes, and priests of Judah: The traditional Tomb of Absalom, opposite the slope of the City of David and on the horizon, Ein Rogel, where David's agents, the priestly scions Ahimaaz and Jonathan, stayed (2 Samuel 17:17). This is also the Byzantine "Hill of Evil Council" where legend says the high priest decided to arrest Jesus.

he remnants of Jerusalem's ancient grandeur teach an important life lesson: nothing is as it seems. David's Tower wasn't built by David. Herod never went through Herod's Gate. No Eastern potentate ever swam in the Sultan's Pool. And Absalom is not buried in Absalom's Tomb.

This magnificent example of tomb architecture, which rises from the depths of the fertile Kidron Valley, was built many centuries after Absalom fled the hills of the Holy City and his father's wrath. But the Bible does say Absalom built a "pillar" in this valley so people would remember him (2 Samuel 18:18) No one knows where that pillar is. And that, as we have said, is how traditions are born.

This tomb is certainly fit for a prince. Its Greek-style architecture reveals it to have been built during the third or second century BC. It may have even been designed for some wealthy and influential local citizen who wanted to await the coming of the Messiah in style. At that very time, people began to realize that when the Messiah came to the Mount of Olives (Zechariah 14:4), the dead buried nearby would be the first to rise from their graves and cross a miraculous bridge to the judgment seat on the Temple Mount. Thus, this part of the Kidron Valley has also been identified as the Valley of *Jehoshaphat*, meaning "the LORD judged" (Joel 3:2, 12.).

Our princely Jerusalemite even had a plaque installed, probably of silver or gold, that must have had

The pyramid-topped tomb of Zechariah, son of Jehoiada, and the tomb of the priestly family of Hezir have been Kidron Valley landmarks for more than 2,000 years.

Absalom's Tomb, showing a gaping hole through which grave robbers long ago sought treasures.

his family's name inscribed on it. One of Jerusalem's great historical ironies is that the only traces of the plaque are four holes for the nails that affixed it to the stone. It was stolen by some ancient grave robber, along with the name this individual tried so hard to preserve.

In the Middle Ages, travelers wrote in their journals about Jews and Muslims throwing stones at the monument and cursing Absalom for rebelling against his father. Over the generations so many stones piled up they almost concealed the tomb, which was excavated in 1925. Alongside the Tomb of Absalom are other tombs, their Doric capitals, pilasters, and other elements revealing that they, too, came from Greek times. One is the traditional Tomb of Zechariah; interestingly not a reference to the prophet so closely associated with the nearby Mount of Olives (see above), but rather the righteous priest Zechariah, son of Jehoiada, who was stoned to death as he chastised the people in the courts of the First Temple (2 Chronicles 24:20–24). Only one tomb, that of a priestly family called the sons of Hezir, can be securely identified as theirs: they inscribed their name on the rock itself, and it survived.

A path leads from Absalom's Tomb to Mount Zion and the Room of the Last Supper in one direction, and to Gethsemane in the other. It follows the very route Jesus would have taken on that Passover night and probably many times before, and it is likely he passed by these very tombs. Perhaps he even gestured toward them, reminding Jerusalemites that all that glitters, so to speak, is far from being gold (Matthew 23:27).

mall. A tiny speck of life on a planet filled with other specks.

And trees. Trees that, in the Kidron Valley, lean as though they are towers in Pisa. Almost straining eastward.

Thick green grasses and ancient bricks walling in an old city with synagogues and churches and mosques where more specks go to pray.

Reaching the Kidron Valley, standing before the place known as Absalom's Tomb, I realize just how small I am and how fleeting life is, especially a life wasted on revenge or one so full of itself that it built such an ostentatious final resting place. This was the valley where David fled from Absalom when his son declared war against the king. This is where images of gods were brought to be burned by kings and priests who loved the Lord.

I have walked all around the tomb, and I peer over my shoulder toward Jerusalem, toward the wall and the one-time gate and dilapidated staircase where Jesus would have exited the city on his way to the Mount of Olives to pray.

To be arrested.

It is no easy walk. The valley is long and steep. Walking from the Mount of Olives to Jerusalem via the valley is one thing. From the city to the mount is another. I wonder, *As he walked along with his chosen disciples, did he pause at the tomb where I now stand? Were there, even then, pock marks from the thrown rocks of the incensed?*

Might Jesus have whispered a prayer to his Father? *They know not what they do.*

O Absalom, my son, my son! (2 Samuel 19:4 NIV) David, in sorrowful anguish, wailed as only a parent can, having learned of the death of a beloved child.

Oh, Jerusalem! Jerusalem! Jesus lamented. *How often I have longed to gather your children together, as a hen gathers her chicks under her wings. . . .* (Matthew 23:37 NIV).

I am forced now to consider what I do not want to think about. My mind wanders where it does not wish to go. It is Judas's words that reverberate in my soul: *Surely not I, Rabbi* (Matthew 26:25 NIV).

Where might I have stood on that day when the crowd called out its words of condemnation against the innocence of Jesus? It's easy to suppose that I would have believed then as I believe now, but I must weigh who I am, my parentage, and my upbringing before I can make such an assumption. Who I am today is a woman who stands in a valley before a pockmarked tomb with the knowledge that the one buried inside is not Absalom at all. Likewise, I can stand before the two places in Jerusalem claiming to be the final resting place of the crucified Jesus and say, "Look! Just as he said! Empty!" because I know the end of the story.

But they did not know. Could not know.

What right do we have, then, to judge the actions of those who respond only to the knowledge they have before them?

Forgive them, Father.

Forgive me.

Right page: *The so-called Tomb of Absalom, with its distinctive pointed roof, was one of the first Jewish burials on the slope of the Mount of Olives, more than 2,000 years ago.*

They went to a place called Gethsemane, and Jesus said to his disciples, "Sit here while I pray." He took Peter, James and John along with him, and he began to be deeply distressed and troubled. "My soul is overwhelmed with sorrow to the point of death," he said to them. "Stay here and keep watch." Going a little farther, he fell to the ground and prayed that if possible the hour might pass from him. "Abba, Father," he said, "everything is possible for you. Take this cup from me. Yet not what I will, but what you will." Then he returned to his disciples and found them sleeping. "Simon," he said to Peter, "are you asleep? Could you not keep watch for one hour? Watch and pray so that you will not fall into temptation. The spirit is willing, but the body is weak." Once more he went away and prayed the same thing. When he came back, he again found them sleeping, because their eyes were heavy. They did not know what to say to him. Returning the third time, he said to them, "Are you still sleeping and resting? Enough! The hour has come. Look, the Son of Man is betrayed into the hands of sinners. Rise! Let us go! Here comes my betrayer!"

Mark 14:32–42 NIV

The Garden of Gethsemane

Ancient olive trees in the Garden of Gethsemane, whose name means "olive oil press."

Every crevice and crack of this gnarled old trunk in the Garden of Gethsemane saw something of Jerusalem's tempestuous history.

arden of Gethsemane—a name that entwines the tragic and the victorious as closely as the woody sinews of the ancient olive trees it contains. *Gethsemane* has come down to us in the Gospels in its Greek form, but it comes from a word in the language Jesus spoke on a daily basis, Aramaic. When Jesus pronounced it, it would have sounded something like this: *gat - SHAMna*. It means [olive] "oil press."

Set aside in your minds the flower garden in your yard, carefully tended to produce beautiful blooms to please the eye and fill the air with fragrance. This garden would have contained *trees that were pleasing to the eye and good for food* (Genesis 2:9 NIV), *beds of spices* (Song of Solomon 6:2), or *herbs* (Luke 11:42). These now-ancient trees might have been young saplings planted to produce the fruit that, when crushed, gave oil for light, food, and even healing.

John, who called this place simply "an olive grove," said Jesus often met here, at the foot of the Mount of Olives, with his disciples. This mountain became known as God's "footstool" (Psalm 132:7), and no wonder: its incomparable view of the Temple on Mount Moriah inspired great teachings, like Jesus' own. During the olive harvest, in the fall, the olives would be beaten until they fell from the trees, and the grove would have thronged with people bringing their olives to be crushed into oil. There, they would have found Jesus, preaching, teaching, and healing. Word would have spread, so that when a man came down the mountain on the back of a white donkey, people shouted *Hosannah* and laid palm branches before him.

But at Passover time, the trees would have been just past flowering, the grove so silent you could almost hear the tiny, pale-green fruit budding. In Jerusalem, bursting with Passover pilgrims, this was a rare place of solitude that Jesus and the disciples would have certainly sought out after their Seder meal, known as the Last Supper.

Christians interpret the pressing of the olives as a symbol of the burden Jesus prayed over, a burden so great that he sweated blood. Overcoming impossible adversity with God's help is a message from Gethsemane's olive trees that shines across the generations. As one ancient Jewish sage put it, Israel is an olive tree, and God is a lamp: "What use is made of olive oil? It is put into a lamp, and then the two together give light as though they were one. Hence the Holy One will say to Israel: My children, since My light is your light and your light is My light, let us go together—you and I—and give light to Zion: "Arise, give light, for thy light has come."[1]

---

1 *Song of Songs Rabbah* 6:10 (ref. Isaiah 60:1).

The Dome of the Rock and the Golden Gate, framed by the olive trees at Dominus Flevit, a chapel marking the site where Jesus wept over Jerusalem (Luke 19:41).

It is not as I pictured it, this garden. Lovely to behold, yes. Even the leaves from ancient trees—gnarled and twisted like an old woman's fingers—shimmer playfully in the day's light. They wave a gentle hello to all who enter, all those who dare to search for the intensity among the beautiful.

But it is not as I pictured.

Flowers bursting in rainbow colors cannot cover the secrets of this place. They hide behind walls and along the roots and the dark gray soil that once absorbed drops of blood from the one who came here to pray. They whisper to all who will quiet their preconceived notions long enough to listen, and I am not here long before I know I want to be one of those who hear.

I slip into a shadow. A chill dances down my spine and—for a moment—time is suspended. A breeze tickles the olive trees, and their leaves rustle, bringing with them the echoes of three men snoring and one man's groan: *Abba.*

This is no longer just a garden; this is the home of the bride. In the age-old tradition, the father comes with his son to offer a lifetime—an eternity—together. "Love me?" the son implores. "And as Jacob loved Rachel, will you allow me to love you?"

The bride is shy and unsure. *What price will he pay?* she wonders. *What bride-price will he offer?*

The son bows his head in anticipation. The price his father has offered is high, but she is worth the price. Isn't she?

"If it be your will, Abba."

The bride blushes. The father pours a cup of wine—the cup of acceptance. *But will she take it? Will she?* Looking up, the son watches with expectation. *Let it pass from me to her,* he prays. *Please, Abba . . . Let her say, "Yes."*

The voices of a throng coming up the Mount of Olives startles. Torches send light

I stand and step out of the shadows and into the light. I reach up, pull an olive branch toward me, and inhale from its leaves. They smell of hope and healing, of bread and wine, of sunlight on a winter's day. Letting go, I turn my face toward Jerusalem and gaze upon the slope of the hills. I reach out, clasp a cup only I can see, and draw it to my lips.

"Yes." I say to the One who hears. "I will be your bride."

Left: A path in the "private garden" across from the traditional Garden of Gethsemane is a place of tranquility.

Left page: The thick trunks of these olive trees in the "private" Garden of Gethsemane show their great age.

slashing into the ink of night. The Bridegroom stands and, looking over his shoulder, slowly turns toward those who believe they are taking him captive.

But he knows what they cannot. You cannot take captive one whose heart is already sold into the slavery of a devotion so deep that no man or woman can begin to comprehend it. They take him from this garden—perhaps from near this very tree where I now sit and ponder—toward Jerusalem. They believe it is by force.

But he knows what they cannot yet know.

It is not the march of the condemned, but the wedding march which has begun.

The metaphor of the "cup" in the Garden of Gethsemane recalls and deepens the symbolism of the four cups of wine of the Passover meal, the *seder*, which Jesus had shared only hours before with his disciples. According to Jewish tradition, the four cups of wine recall the four stages of redemption God describes in Exodus 6:6–7. In literal translation from the Hebrew, these stages are: "I will take you out . . ."; "I will save you . . ."; "I will redeem you . . ."; and "I will take you as my nation."

*P*ilate handed Jesus over to them to be crucified. The soldiers took charge of Jesus. Carrying his own cross, Jesus went out to a place called The Place of the Skull, which in the Hebrew language is called Golgotha. There they crucified Jesus. They also crucified two other men, one on each side, with Jesus in the middle.

John 19:16–18

Via Dolorosa

Modern-day "daughters of Jerusalem" on the Via Dolorosa, one of Jerusalem's main market streets, then and now.

The well-loved George Bernard hymn about Jesus' crucifixion in Jerusalem that begins "On a hill far away . . . " has influenced three generations of Christians as they picture Jesus on the way to Calvary. But where in the Holy City is the winding pathway to be found, shaded by old olive trees and cypresses, leading up hill and down dale to a horizon on which the dark silhouette of three crosses stand? This is the question visitors to Jerusalem often ask as they are led through crowded alleyways, centuries-old houses rising up on either side, and city markets with vendors hawking mint and oregano, fresh-killed fish, olive-wood carvings, and crucifixes in a dozen languages. *How,* they wonder, *can this be the way to Calvary?*

Some are surprised to find out that the Via Dolorosa ("the way of sorrow"), this modern version of the route Jesus took bearing the cross, might be a more faithful reflection of the ancient one than anything evoked by our imagination. In those days, crucifixion was the Romans' method of choice to execute their political enemies. A cruel form of death, which took hours if not days to release its victims, the Romans used it not only to eliminate the condemned but to terrorize the living. Thus, crucifixions were carried out not on distant hills, but as close to the city as possible, to remind the inhabitants of the horrific price to pay for crossing Rome.

Forcing the condemned man to carry the crossbeam through the streets was part of the punishment and its deterrent power. Here was the victim, close enough to touch, inching agonizingly past the market stall; vendors scrambling away from his path with their piles of herbs on the curbside, shoppers shifting their burdens from one shoulder to the other as they pull their child out of the way.

Nowadays, in tourism's "high season" during Easter and Passover, Old Jerusalem's roads teem with people from all over the world, flowing along main streets like the Via Dolorosa, spilling into its alleys, eddying around

The theater in Verona, the Coliseum, and Titus' Arch in Rome—these are only a few of the impressive remains of Roman domination that are part and parcel of their modern cities, an unending flow of traffic eddying around them. In Jerusalem, present-day visitors have practically no clue of the ruins, hidden by later civilizations until discovered by recent generations. The First Station of the Cross, in the basement of the Sisters of Zion Convent in the Old City, is such a site. In the nineteenth century, the sisters identified the remains of a late Roman arch as the site where Pontius Pilate presented Jesus to the crowd. They were mistaken about the date of the arch, but beneath the convent they built, they indeed found remains of the huge Antonia Fortress, very likely the place of Pilate's judgment, where Jesus took up the Cross.

A market street in Jerusalem, draped with merchandise and tongue-in-cheek advertising for a coffee shop like no other in the world.

the market stalls, calling to each other when they spy a bargain, turning every scene into an object to be photographed.

People have been taking this walk since Byzantine times, but today's Via Dolorosa was set in stone by medieval times, when the Fourteen Stations of the Cross came into being. Some of the Stations are based on the gospel account. The Fifth Station, where Simon of Cyrene helped Jesus carry the cross, is now located across the street from a photography store. Others, like Station Six where Veronica wiped Jesus' brow with her veil or the three stations marking Jesus' falling with the cross, come from sacred legend. The last four stations are not in the street at all, but within the Church of the Holy Sepulchre.

The Roman crucifixions have ended, but peoples' desire to walk in Jesus' footsteps means the streets have changed precious little since his time.

A Muslim girl gets the best view of the crowd on a typical market day on the Via Dolorosa. The doorway of the chapel of the Fifth Station, marking the traditional place where Simon of Cyrene helped Jesus carry the cross, is in the background.

I've heard it said that the Via Dolorosa—the Way of Sorrows—is a walk of faith and remembering rather than a walk of history. It is a method by which Christians commemorate that Jesus came, was condemned, flogged nearly to death, then—with a crossbeam laid across his shoulders—struggled through the streets of Jerusalem toward a hill where, stripped, he would die hanging above his beloved city. The stops—stations, they are called—between St. Stephen's Gate and the Church of the Holy Sepulchre bring everything to mind in vivid color and in surround sound.

Jerusalem heaves with people from all nations and religions. Individuals grasp hold of what they can by sight and sound, and they worship—whether quietly or in the midst of a multitude's cacophony.

Streets go from wide and open to narrow and nearly suffocating in places . . . so much so that I nearly inhale the head covering of the woman walking in front of me. The blended smells of sweat and spices are intoxicating. They are caught in the music and hawking from the market stalls, and they swirl around me. For a moment I forget where I am, where I am going, even the steps he took as I burst out in laughter. There is excitement in the streets of Jerusalem. Life exudes from every shop, every cheaply and expensively made souvenir, every young man selling tapestry bags, and every old woman selling her herbs and vegetables. They are Jerusalem's pulse, and this street its artery.

Though driven forward and toward the last of the stations, I am moved more by the first than the last. From here, and peering over crowds and buildings as best I can, my eyes search for the familiar dome of the Church of the Holy Sepulchre. It is, I decide, a long way from here to there.

Not so much in distance, but in time. From the beginning of time until the moment he stood before the crowds, this was the plan.

What measure of the Divine is this that we adore and serve?

A haunting melody comes to mind, and my soul sings.

What wondrous love is this, O my soul, O my
    soul!
What wondrous love is this that caused the
    Lord of bliss
To bear the dreadful curse for my soul, for my
    soul?

To God and to the Lamb, I will sing, I will sing;
To God and to the Lamb who is the great "I
    Am";
While millions join the theme, I will sing.
And when from death I'm free, I'll sing on, I'll
    sing on;
And when from death I'm free, I'll sing and
    joyful be;
And through eternity, I'll sing on.[1]

---

1 Alexander Means, "What Wondrous Love Is This?" Music from *The Southern Harmony and Musical Companion* by William Walker (New York: Hastings House, 1835).

The rooftops of Jerusalem's Old City around the black-domed church of the Holy Sepulchre seem almost to touch, leaving room for only the narrowest lanes to traverse below.

I rejoiced with those who said to me, "Let us go to the house of the Lord." Our feet are standing in your gates, O Jerusalem. Jerusalem is built like a city that is closely compacted together. That is where the tribes go up, the tribes of the Lord, to praise the name of the Lord according to the statute given to Israel. There the thrones for judgment stand, the thrones of the house of David.

Pray for the peace of Jerusalem: "May those who love you be secure. May there be peace within your walls and security within your citadels." For the sake of my brothers and friends, I will say, "Peace be within you." For the sake of the house of the Lord our God, I will seek your prosperity.

Psalm 122 NIV

Church of the Holy Sepulchre

Pillars of their faith, Armenian Orthodox acolytes await their priests at the doorway of the Holy Sepulchre.

233

ome Christians say they feel more comfortable picturing the tomb of Jesus in the Garden Tomb, a setting where visitors can still behold all the elements of the story: Golgotha, and nearby the tomb, the garden. The dappled beauty of the Garden Tomb, first regarded as the tomb of Jesus in the nineteenth century, contrasts sharply with the ancient Church of the Holy Sepulchre's dark, cavernous interior, cold marble floors, and mysterious winding staircases. Its tomb is no longer rock-cut, but rather a stone structure inside the church rotunda, inscribed with Cyrillic letters dating back to the days of Russian Orthodox control. At present, six denominations cautiously share sacred condominium here, precisely mapped out over the centuries, not only room by room, but down to the middle of a column, a window ledge, or a step. To some it might seem that the only thing to recommend this

A view of St. Vartan's Chapel, deep beneath the Church of the Holy Sepulchre.

The keys to the Church of the Holy Sepulchre appear a number of times in history and lore. According to one tradition, the Muslim Caliph Harun al-Rashid (786–809) of "Arabian Nights" fame, gave the key to Emperor Charlemagne, the defining force in early ninth-century Christian Europe, as Charlemagne negotiated for protection of the Christians under the Muslims. After the fall of Crusader Jerusalem in 1246, Sultan As-Salib Ayoub awarded the key to one Muslim family, and the right to open the door to anther. The descendents of the Judeh and the Insaibe families still retain the key* and open the door ceremonially every Easter Eve before a crowd of thousands and the world media.

*Saul P. Colbi, *A History of Christian Presence in the Holy Land* (Lanham, MD: University Press of America, 1988). 52.

building, which has been called the most complex building in the world, is its unusual architecture and history.

But for those seeking a bond with other Christians from the first century to this day, bridging the unfamiliarity of their celebration of the faith, this might be the best place to begin. Down a long staircase, whose walls are covered with tiny crosses etched over hundreds of years by thousands of pilgrims, deep below the church, is a First Temple-era stone quarry. The quarry left a huge cavern, where tradition says

A rare photograph of the "Boat Inscription" deep beneath the Church of the Holy Sepulchre, carved by early Christian pilgrims. The inscription reads: Domine Ivimus (Lord we shall go) and is carved into the rock of the First Temple quarry.

the cross of Jesus was miraculously found by Queen Helene, whose son, the first Christian emperor Constantine, built the church in the early fourth century. At these foundations of the structure, with which Constantine replaced the pagan shrine Hadrian thought could obviate Christianity, the first of the faithful ever to have worshipped here may have left behind a trace of their existence—an engraving.

It was discovered in 1971 in the Armenian Chapel of St. Vartan behind the great cavern. On one smooth stone, now preserved under glass and visible only to those who can persuade the Armenians to unlock the door, is the carving of a ship, about 26 inches long and 12 inches high. Beneath it, two Latin words can be seen: *Domine Ivimus*, believed to be a version of Psalm 122:1,

meaning "Lord we shall go." The ship, scholars say, is a Roman merchant vessel in harbor (Caesarea?), with its mainmast apparently broken.[1] The ship's design and the inscription date it to the first or second century AD. It may have been incised on the Hadrianic wall, before the church of the Holy Sepulchre was built, by a Christian pilgrim who nearly perished on a sea journey to Jerusalem and was thus giving thanks for safe haven.[2] We will never know for sure. But in this mystery is certainly a gift with the power to forge a rare and precious bond between today's Christians and those of the distant past.

---

1 Shimon Gibson and Joan Taylor, *Beneath the Church of the Holy Sephuchre* (London: Palestine Exploration Fund, 1994), 35.

2 Professor Dan Bahat, personal communication, May 2007.

Reflections

he doorway of the church boasts of a steady stream of pilgrims. The arches overhead are as elegantly shaped as a woman's brow. Though the beige stones of the courtyard before it are washed in sunlight, there is a brooding darkness from inside. Still people pour in and out of it like wine in and out of a chalice.

Inside, we are met by those who kneel at the marble stone where, it is said, Jesus was anointed for burial. It seems stained by a deep red dripping from its sides. Overhead, eight ornamental lamps hang like pendulums.

Bypassing the station, we slip into a room where my friend speaks in whispered tones to a priest. I try to read his response to her plea, but his face holds no expression.

Above: *An Armenian Orthodox service in the part of the Holy Sepulchre in their charge, marking the site where the angel showed the women Jesus' empty tomb, depicted in a painting on the wall behind them.*

Yet, before I can think of what we are about to do here—so different from those who have entered this day—we are being hurried out the door. The priest holds in his hand a key, and his feet drum a rhythm against the stone flooring.

Quickly.

I am slipping into mysterious passageways, allowing my hand to steady my body by momentarily pressing against lofty columns as we round them. My heart is exploding within my chest. As we pass by, observing pilgrims appear like unpainted pickets of a fence beside a road. Their heads turn after us, wondering—no doubt—where we are heading in such a rush.

I feel a recent injury along my Achilles' heel reopen; blood trickles into my shoe. I don't care; rather, I push myself harder to keep up.

Quickly!

We skip down a dark stairwell; I feel as though we are descending to the very core of the earth. The back of my friend's head becomes a blur; the priest is but a shadow within a shadow.

We are led into a small chapel. There is a table before us where three candles flicker. They are the room's only light, and the three of us—the priest, my Jewish friend, and me—are the only people. I hear the jangling of keys; I follow the sound. The priest stands at an iron gate before a steel door. He unlocks them both, then turns to us again.

Quickly.

We pass through the doorway, down more steps, and into a well-guarded chapel. My friend points to a small opening in the wall. *Through here.* I duck my head and enter in. The room is cold, damp. Deeper still within the earth. Rounding another corner, I stop. There it is: a drawing carved into the quarry rock by hands that came this way nearly seventeen hundred years ago. I collapse to the floor before it, willing my heart to return to its normal pulse. But I cannot. *It* cannot. *Domine Ivimus.*

What drew the pilgrims from the boat to this place beneath Jerusalem so long ago? What draws *me* now?

The boat holds the answer, I think. I must—as those who came before—behold what has always existed with my own eyes. Touch it with my own hands. I must worship the one who, like those who shuffle in and out of the cavernous rooms above me, poured himself out like wine from a chalice. I must love his city and his land.

And I must risk it all to do so.

The dome over the tomb structure in the inner sanctum of the Church of the Holy Sepuchre.

*I*f my people, who are
called by my name, will humble
themselves and pray and seek
my face and turn from their
wicked ways, then will I hear
from heaven and will forgive
their sin and will heal their land.

2 Chronicles 7:14 NIV

The Western Wall

*A view of the Western Wall, the prayer plaza, the golden Dome of
the Rock, and the Mount of Olives in the background.*

hat draws pilgrims, Jews and Christians from all over the world, to the Western Wall? As sacred as it is said to be, one might think this remnant of the Temple of Jesus' time must have been the very inner wall of the Holy of Holies. But it was not. It was the western retaining wall, one of four Herod the Great built to support the gargantuan plaza on which he raised the Temple, which was the greatest building project in the Roman world. The dimensions are indeed amazing; the portion where people pray is only 187 feet out of its total length of approximately 1,455 feet; its remaining 62 feet of height are only about two-thirds of the height the original soared. It even reached some 60 feet below ground level.[1]

These are fascinating details. But the answer to the question with which we started comes not in focusing on how deep below ground the wall goes, but how deep into the heart, and why.

God told Ezekiel the space around the Temple would always remain holy (Ezekiel 43:12). These words were never forgotten, and sometime after the Romans destroyed the Temple in AD 70, perhaps in the dark days following the Jews' failed second attempt to throw off Roman rule (the Bar Kokhba Revolt in AD 135), Jewish sages sought to remind their flock that God had not

Above: Dress code is not an issue when it's prayer time at the Western Wall.

---

1 Meir Ben-Dov, *In the Shadow of the Temple* (Jerusalem: Keter 1984), 77, 87.

abandoned them. The deeper meaning behind the Song of Solomon 2:9: *Look, he stands behind our wall*, they said, meant "the Almighty stands behind the [Western] Wall from where he keeps vigil."[2]

Many sources say the *Shekhinah*, that part of God whose name comes from the word "dwelling" and who dwells within us, never departed from this place.

When Solomon dedicated the Temple, he asked God to hear the prayers not only of Israelites, but of all who have "come from a distant land because of your name" (1 Kings 8:41 NIV). Solomon knew a building could not hold God (1 Kings 8:27), just as we know that God is not in these stones. But God dwells in us as we touch them.

---

2 Nahmanides commentary *on Song of Songs Rabbah* 2:24. Quoted in Zev Vilnay, *Legends of Jerusalem* (Philadelphia: The Jewish Publication Society, 1973), 166.

God is in this place. In fact, in the sacred meeting point between the Almighty and human beings, Jewish tradition says God *is* "Place." God is where we are as the Jews grieve over the loss of the Temple; God is where we are in the joy of the return to the Western Wall after Jerusalem was reunited; God is in the proud eyes of parents who raised their son to want to read from the Torah for the first time at his Bar Mitzvah here; God watches the soldiers who take their oath of loyalty on the Bible here. God is in every prayer of supplication uttered here for hundreds of years.

Come here. Touch the stones. And feel the *Place*.

A boy is joyfully carried aloft at the Western Wall after becoming Bar Mitzvah—a son of the commandments.

am filled with inexplicable joy!

We approach the wall early on Monday morning, and I am filled with anticipation. Mondays, my Jewish friend tells me, is a day when boys become men at the Western Wall of Jerusalem. Here, she tells me, a bar mitzvah might be taking place.

We are still a long way off when we hear the singing and the elation that accompanies it. It pulsates toward us, and we are pulled to it as though we have no choice but to go. But there are rules and, as women, we are only allowed so far.

I am enclosed by a crowd of onlookers—women who ululate from their side of the wall before throwing sweets to the men. Finding a place to stand, I stretch tall to witness the ceremony. The *shofar* is blown and the Torah is raised as men lift a now-teenaged boy—full of hope and glee—to the level of their shoulders. He bobs up and down in a time-honored tradition as those who have passed this way before link arms over shoulders and dance informally. The women ululate again, and the men turn, anxious for the candy the women will throw. It is a privilege to be here. It is delight in its purest form for both God and his creation.

"Siman tov! Mazal tov!"

I step away from the festivities and inch my way toward the large stones of the wall where women pray. *Tzetels*—prayers written on small pieces of paper— are jammed within the cracks, packed like cotton in a wound. This is, they say, the shortest route to God's ear.

I square my shoulders, confident that I know differently . . . *better,* in fact. The shortest route to God's ear, I think, is my knees. But when in Rome . . .

An odd thought, I know, seeing as Romans destroyed all but what is left here. But not this wall. And not prayer to God. Try as they may, as long as God stirs the hearts of his children, no one will ever destroy that.

Men at the Western Wall celebrate a bar mitzvah with joyful dance.

much about prayer—about God—about how he hears the prayers of his children.

Here, I realize, I know nothing at all.

Corrected and spent, I step away as I was earlier instructed to do: not turning my back right away. There is a shifting in the crags over where I had stood, and I stop and stare.

A perfect white dove looks down on me from his perch, then, stretching his wings, flies away.

Left: *How many fervent prayers have young women sent heavenward from here over the centuries?*

Below: *"And furthermore..." A gentleman speaks to the Creator of the Universe at the Western Wall, amid prayer notes placed there by the faithful.*

Slipping between the clusters of women who weep in travail, I am finally in a position to stretch my arm between shoulders that curve and sway toward the wall. My fingertips graze the cold stone; what feels like an electrical shock shoots through my body. It is so completely unexpected; my knees buckle. My fingers curl in an attempt to hold on to nothing more than a crack. Pulling myself up, I press my face into the wall and begin to sob. I don't understand this. I thought I knew so

*L*ater, Joseph from Arimathea asked Pilate if he could take the body of Jesus. (Joseph was a secret follower of Jesus, because he was afraid of the leaders.) Pilate gave his permission, so Joseph came and took Jesus' body away. Nicodemus, who earlier had come to Jesus at night, went with Joseph. He brought about seventy-five pounds of myrrh and aloes. These two men took Jesus' body and wrapped it with the spices in pieces of linen cloth, which is how they bury the dead. In the place where Jesus was crucified, there was a garden. In the garden was a new tomb that had never been used before. The men laid Jesus in that tomb because it was nearby, and they were preparing to start their Sabbath day.

John 19:38–42

Very early on the first day of the week, at dawn, the women came to the tomb, bringing the spices they had prepared. They found the stone rolled away from the entrance of the tomb, but when they went in, they did not find the body of the Lord Jesus. While they were wondering about this, two men in shining clothes suddenly stood beside them. The women were very afraid and bowed their heads to the ground. The men said to them, "Why are you looking for a living person in this place for the dead?"

Luke 24:1–5

The Garden Tomb

A view of the Garden Tomb, where thousands come every year to celebrate the empty chamber.

The Garden Tomb is not only the source of some of the most powerful memories Christians have of Jerusalem, but it also reflects a slice of the Holy City of bygone days and some of its colorful figures.[1]

Perhaps the most famous of these is Major General Charles George Gordon (1833–1885), after whom the Garden Tomb is nicknamed "Gordon's Calvary." But as with most of Jerusalem, things are not always what they seem.

The military feats and administrative talents of Gordon, a Royal Engineer, spanned three continents. In the wake of his campaigns in China, he was nicknamed "Chinese" Gordon. He served with the Egyptian army and was for a time the governor of Sudan. Sent by the British to rescue Egyptian dependents from an uprising in Sudan in 1884, Gordon was caught in the siege in Khartoum, where he died on January 26, 1885.

Between an appointment in Mauritius in 1882 and a request by the Belgian king to administer the Congo, Gordon spent about a year in the Holy Land. He lived in Ein Karem but was a frequent guest of the Spafford family in their Old City home. A year or so before Gordon came to Jerusalem, Horatio and Anna Spafford settled here following the loss of their four daughters in a shipwreck. Spafford is remembered as the author of the hymn, "It Is well (with My Soul)," penned after this tragedy.

From the roof of the Spafford house near Damascus Gate, Gordon could see the outcropping already known as Skull Hill, according to a letter he wrote to a friend.

---

1 Information for this chapter came from Bill White's book *A Special Place* (Grantham, U: Stanborough Press, 1989).

Watchful eyes seem to peer from the rock overlooking the Garden Tomb, evoking the meaning of the name Golgotha—Skull.

It takes little imagination to see the "eyes" of the skull in this rocky outcropping visible over the fence from the Garden Tomb.

He visited the site the morning after he arrived in Jerusalem and eventually came to believe this to be the likely site of the crucifixion. He never mentions the existence of a tomb here although according to explorer C.R. Conder, it had been excavated a decade before. But by 1892, according to a letter in *The Times*, it had become known as "Gordon's Tomb," and proposals were made to purchase it.

The Garden Tomb was eventually purchased thanks to the efforts of two women: Louisa Hope and Charlotte Hussey. Hussey, a Jerusalem missionary, wrote that Hope had often spoken to her about efforts to purchase the tomb from another famous Jerusalem figure, the German banker Johannes Frutiger. Thanks to Hussey's acquaintance with Mrs. Frutiger, and after the land was surveyed by Jerusalem architect Conrad Schick, Hope and Hussey formed a committee, raised the funds, and after many vicissitudes, purchased the land in May 1898.

Although the Garden is closely associated with the British, notably, the Garden's first caretaker was Danish carpenter and adventurer, Peder Beckholdt, who was part of the expedition organized by Henry Morton Stanley to find David Livingston in Africa. This postscript reminds us that the Garden Tomb is, from that day to this, beloved by Christians all over the world.

Reflections

e enter in, greeted by an array of well-tended flora and fauna. They burst with color or song, according to their being . . . their call in life. There is a coolness here, even in the heat of day. It draws me along paths carved into the rocky earth and dotted in hues of buds and blooms. I walk behind a man named Peter, and within moments I am face-to-face with what appears to be—across the way—the skull of a tormented soul formed along the side of a hill and look-

ing down upon Jerusalem's Damascus Gate. I stay only a while, then I move toward that which brings people from all over the world.

The tomb.

There are places to sit outside the tomb, and so I do. I think what it must have been like to have been Mary from Magdala, loving Jesus as she did, seeing him die, and watching them remove his torn body from the cross for preparation.

She followed close enough to see where they took him, to watch them from opposite the tomb, sitting—perhaps—where I am now. As she wept—for surely she wept—did her breath, I wonder, catch in her throat? Did she hold herself back from entering that tomb, caring for the one she loved and who loved her? Did she collapse, inconsolable, when they rolled the stone into its place? Did Joseph of Arimathea, perhaps, shuffle to her, extend a hand, and say, "It's over. Let's go"?

But it wasn't over. In the end, Mary could not stay away from the tomb any more than Jesus could stay in it. Leaving before dawn, Mary slipped along the streets of Jerusalem until she came to his tomb, arriving just as sunlight shot through the leaves of trees and commanded blooms of flowers to spread their petals wide.

Why do you seek the living among the dead?

I look down at my own hands and imagine hers, carrying death's spices, dropping them to the ground beneath her feet. Fear and faith collide.

Didn't he say it would be so?

Why, then, the spices? Had she not believed? Human, after all, she could only grasp with her heart what her eyes could see. She'd had faith enough to follow but not enough to believe. She only knew for certain what she had *seen* but doubted what she had *heard*.

"Mary," spoke the one she believed to be the gardener.

"Rabboni."

She cannot hold on to him, though it is all she wants to do. She must tell others. *I have seen the Lord!*

There is before me a tomb surrounded by resplendent gardens. Some say it is the burial place of Jesus; others say it is not. At the caretaker's leading, I stand and take the necessary steps toward it. I place my hand on the rough wall around the cave's opening, dip my head, and peer inside. Then I enter; but I cannot stay, though staying in this loveliness is all I want to do. Instead, I must tell others. The tomb is empty.

It is beautiful, and it is empty.

Many believe the forbidding Skull Hill, where a Muslim cemetery now stands, to have been the ancient execution site where the cross of Jesus was placed. His cross, along with those of many other unfortunates murdered by Jerusalem's Roman overlords, would have been in a high spot that could easily be seen, with the execution acting as a warning. This site may have had additional meaning for Jerusalemites of Jesus' day. A cave on the slope of Skull Hill, now inside of a mosque, preserves an ancient legend: It is, they say, the prison in which Jeremiah was thrown by King Zedekiah's officials in order to stop his preaching the impending doom of the Babylonian conquest (Jeremiah 37:15).

Left page: The morning sun illuminates the doorway in the rock-cut façade of the Garden Tomb.

Miriam's Farewell: At the End of Our Journey

his is not the "conclusion" because from your first experience of touching the Bible, whether from your armchair at home or among the rocky ruins and people of its land, you will never want to stop.

As Eva Marie and I traveled Israel together, I saw that marvelous transformation happen in the mind and heart of a person of faith—the same transformation that has been my privilege to see happen countless times to Christians I have accompanied. I saw the "aha" moments, the light go on in her eyes as she puts the sites, sounds, fragrances, and feelings together with verses she had studied and prayed about and taught to others. I felt Eva's quietude as I sat by the Sea of Galilee some distance away and watched her pick her way across the rocks and take her place by the water. I felt my friend's excitement as she flipped open her Bible purposely a dozen times a day and pored over it. "Wait a minute—I just thought of something," she would say, never failing to find the verse she sought like a human concordance. I will forever hear that voice, sharing with me gems of Scripture discovered or rediscovered in the land. I will forever be grateful to her for allowing me to voice the thoughts that have come to me at many precious sites for more than three decades. Knowing that Eva sees this land as her home, too, makes me honor what it represents all the more.

I felt Eva's thrill at the Western Wall, and I sensed that she and I were not alone before these ancient stones. I don't mean the hundreds of women that surrounded us, some praying silently, some mouthing the words like Hannah at Shiloh, some silently weeping. It was the same sense I get on Yom Kippur, the "Day of Atonement," as I stand in the synagogue, listening to chanting of the solemn Kol Nidre prayer that ushers in day; it was the same feeling I get around the Passover table when we read: "Each of us must see ourselves as if we personally were led out of Egypt." It was the feeling that I represented, at that moment, generations of the Jewish people of whom I am a part, reaching back into the past and going forward into the future. And I felt blessed that I am part of a generation that can stand at the Western Wall together with another whose path may seem different, but is ultimately the same.

Falling into the Bible in the Holy Land together with Eva Marie meant a meeting of minds and hearts on common ground—common holy ground. The Bible is our common book, we said to each other so many times. So many stories—from Miriam leading the Israelites in praise by the Red Sea or mourned by them in the desolate Tzin Valley, to Mary drawing her water in Nazareth or trembling on a mountaintop for the fate of her child; from the recorded and unknown healings Jesus performed at the Sea of Galilee, to the grand monuments of the generations—speak powerfully to both of us. We are from different places and have taken different paths, but we share a great and firm foundation strong enough to hold us all.

It is my deepest wish for you that from these pages, and someday when you touch the Bible yourselves in the land, you will find the renewal of spirit promised by Scripture. You will be turning bookmarks into landmarks for the rest of your life.

Acknowledgements, Toda, and Thank You!

Yihiyu leratzion imrei fi, vehegiyon libi lifanecha, Adonai, tzuri vegoali. Amen.

May the words of my mouth and the meditations of my heart be acceptable unto Thee, my rock and my redeemer. Amen. (Psalm 19:14)

There are many to thank for this book; we're not really sure where to begin. First and foremost, a huge thank-you to God, who brought two women together in Israel and then gave them a calling—a job to do, if you will. We have not only shared great intimacies with him there, but we have come to love each other deeply and with much respect.

Mr. el Heib, without you, dear man, this book would not exist. It was your words, prompted by God inside your heart, that led to Eva Marie's "fall" and with that fall the birth of a book idea! *Toda* for allowing us—and the world—to *fall into the Bible.*

Thank you to Crosswalk.com for running Eva Marie's articles about Israel back in 2002. Your part in this has not gone unnoticed.

Toda to our friends and loved ones in Israel:

Doron Nissim, photographer extraordinaire! *Toda* for the use of your fabulous photographs and for teaching us "the answer to all questions: Photoshop!" You are a true genius, not only with your camera but with your words, for it was you who said, "Follow the light. If you follow the light, you will always get the best picture." We wonder if you know just how brilliant you are.

To Yael Volberg, graphic artist, who introduced us to Doron's work.

To our precious "Rose" at Deck's Restaurant on the Sea of Galilee in Tiberias. You spoiled us with food, song, and dance as we dined in your fabulous not-to-be-missed establishment. The evenings we spent with you will forever be among our best memories. May your doors be blessed with the hungry—not only for your cuisine but for your vivacious spirit and loving heart—and their tummies and souls filled with good things!

To Peter Wells and Liz Woods of the Garden Tomb, for their assistance in providing unusual information about the Garden.

To Alex Barak of the Jesus Boat Museum. *Toda* for the coffee and for your years of love and friendship. A special "Shalom" to your lovely wife, Tova, and to your partners, Ohad and Naama Harpaz. We love you all so much! As you greet those who enter your doorway, may you be blessed as richly as you are a blessing to others!

To Marina Banai of the Jesus Boat Museum. *Toda* for your help with the photos of the Man of Galilee boat.

To Zueira Barakat, who cares for the church in Nain and welcomed us so warmly.

To Pastor Denny Stahl for inspiration at Ein Gedi.

To the staff of Nof Ginnosar Guest House for your warm hospitality and greetings upon our arrival!

To the kind staff at Yardenit, the baptismal site on the Jordan River. *Toda* for taking time to serve and speak with us.

To Dov and Moshe Kempinski of Shorashim of the Old City Biblical Shop in Jerusalem. Talking with you about the deeper things of God was a highlight of our time together.

A special thanks goes to Maya Vamosh, our "cover girl," and her fiancé, Yonatan Dubinsky, for taking the photo and to Nili Vamosh for her facilitation of our deadline.

Finally, to the young lady who helped Eva Marie buy *Naot* sandals at Khalifa Shoes on Jaffa Street in Jerusalem. She could not have taken another step without you!

Thank you to Eva Marie's brother, Van Purvis, for use of his mega-expensive camera. We know that was truly a sacrifice and a decision you must have sweated over for the weeks Eva Marie was away!

Thank you to Jessica Everson, Eva Marie's daughter, who learned Photoshop and did such a fabulous job with our photography!

Thank you to Debbie Wickwire, editor at Thomas Nelson, who originally saw the value of this book and of our working together. Thank you to our vast number of publishers, editors, and associates at Thomas Nelson: Mark Whitlock, Ramona Richards, Karen Artl, Wayne Hastings, the list goes on and on . . . .

Thank you to Robin Crosslin, who took a manuscript and a bunch of photographs and produced the work of art that became this book.

Thank you to our agent, Deidre Knight of The Knight Agency.

Thank you to all who prayed for us while we worked on this project, especially Eva Marie's AWSA sisters.

Thank you to those who traveled with us in 2002: Mina Ganem of the Israel Ministry of Tourism, who spearheaded the trip and the IMOT staff, as well as Rebekah Montgomery, Cate Savidge, Christin Ditchfield, Sandy Bloomfield, Virelle Kidder, Dana Kempler, and one heck of a driver, Nachshon Zada.

And finally, but most especially, *thank you and toda* to our husbands, Dennis Everson and Arik Vamosh. We love you!

Dana Kempler
(1957-2007)
Israel 2002

Photo Credits

Left: *Eva Marie Everson*
Below: *Miriam Feinberg Vamosh*

Yigal Allon Center
   (The Man of Galilee Museum):
153, 155, 156

Palphot Ltd., Israel
69, 73, 74, 76

Doron Nissim:
23, 27, 32, 47, 49 (and insert), 67, 71, 81, 82, 85 (and insert), 108, 109, 138, 162,167, 169, 209, 227, 230, 233, 236, 237, 239, 240, 243 (insert)

Miriam Feinberg Vamosh:
xi, 15, 19, 20, 43, 53, 61, 99, 102, 107, 114, 115, 135, 137, 139, 141, 163, 184, 191, 192, 193, 195, 199 (insert), 225, 231, 245, 247, 248, 254

Eva Marie Everson:
17, 19 (insert), 21, 24, 25, 26, 27 (insert), 29, 31, 31 (insert), 33, 35, 36, 37 (and insert), 38, 39 (and insert), 41, 44, 45 (and insert), 50, 51, 55, 56, 57 (2), 59, 62, 63, 64, 65, 79, 83, 84, 87, 88, 90, 91, 93, 95, 96, 97, 100, 101 (and insert), 103 (and insert), 105, 111, 112, 113, 117, 119 (and insert), 120, 121, 123, 124, 126, 127, 129, 131, 132, 133, 143, 144, 145, 147, 148, 149, 150, 151, 159, 160, 161 (and insert), 165, 166, 171, 172, 173, 175, 177, 178, 179, 181, 183, 185 (and insert), 186, 187, 189, 197, 199, 200, 201, 203, 204, 205, 206, 207, 210, 211 (and insert), 213, 215, 216, 217, 219, 221, 222, 223, 224, 229, 234, 235, 241, 242, 243, 246, 253, 254

Notes